INTRODUCING

Melanie

Klein

Robert Hinshelwood, Susan Robinson
and Oscar Zarate

Edited by Richard Appignanesi

TOTEM BOOKS

First published in the United States in 1998 by Totem Books
Inquiries to PO Box 223, Canal Street Station
New York, NY 10013

Distributed to the trade in the United States
by National Book Network Inc.,
4720 Boston Way, Lanham, Maryland 20706

Text copyright © 1997 Robert Hinshelwood and Susan Robinson
Illustrations copyright © 1997 Oscar Zarate

Originating editor: Richard Appignanesi

ISBN 1 874166 61 7

Library of Congress Catalog Card Number: 97-060792

Printed and bound in Great Britain by
Biddles Ltd., Guildford and King's Lynn

Introducing Melanie Klein

Melanie Klein's work was always uncompromising. She was determined to get to the most hidden "depths" of the human mind. Because she often unearthed such challenging aspects of ourselves, her writing might seem at first difficult and upsetting. She was aware that the concealed terrors and bliss of infancy would not find easy acceptance. "Description of such primitive processes suffers from a great handicap. These phantasies arise at a time when the infant has not yet begun to think in words." Nevertheless, she believed that the health of the human race in the future depended on these levels of the mind becoming accessible and accepted.

**We must look to the future
by seeing that child analysis is
part of all primary education.**

Melanie's Childhood

Born on 30 March 1882 in Vienna, Melanie felt unwanted as the youngest of the four children of Dr Moriz Reizes and Libussa Deutsch. Her father was orthodox Jewish, had been married before, and was 24 years older than Libussa, a reported beauty. He was not a particularly successful general practitioner.

Libussa, out of keeping with the times, ran a shop for a while. Their children, Emilie born 1876, Emanuel in 1877, Sidonie in 1878, and Melanie, were all destined to have either brief or difficult lives. Sidonie died of tuberculosis aged eight (Melanie was then four), and Emanuel too died of tuberculosis, but at the age of twenty-five. Emilie survived childhood, but made a poor marriage to an alcoholic gambler.

Early Sorrows

Melanie, the only child not breast-fed by mother, had a wet nurse. Her father openly favoured Emilie. Clearly this start could have influenced Melanie in her desire to make sense of child development and depression.

Her psychoanalytic contributions uniquely stressed the raw, painful emotions of rage, envy and hatred as well as creativity, and she attributed such powerful feelings to children. She particularly stressed the very earliest relationship of all – to the mother's breast.

Education and Marriage

Melanie longed for her father's approval, and above all to achieve this through intellectual success. She entered the Vienna Gymnasium at sixteen and hoped to become a doctor like him. This changed when he died two years later in 1900. Emilie, recently wed, moved into the household with her alcoholic husband Leo Pick who continued the medical practice and supported the family. Libussa was a young and energetic widow.

Next she sent Emanuel, ill with tuberculosis and addicted to drugs and alcohol, off to travel in Europe and pursue his ideal of a young sick artist.

A Destiny of Travel

Three months after the death of her brother Emanuel in December 1902, she married Arthur. This resulted in continual travelling in connection with his job as an engineer. A year later, in 1904, Melanie's first child Melitta was born. She nursed the baby for seven months, until Arthur's work took them both away and Melitta was cared for by Libussa and nannies.

The notion of travel as an antidote to depression seems to have been strong in the family and may have contributed to some of Melanie's later significant moves. For the two-and-a-half years that the Kleins lived in Silesia, Melanie was more often than not away.

SHE WAS ABSENT FOR PERHAPS THE MOST SIGNIFICANT AND DRAMATIC MOMENTS IN THE LIVES OF HER TWO OLDER CHILDREN.

One may wonder if Melanie's sense of guilt and loss at missing these early years, and at being emotionally unavailable due to her depression, led her later to "experiment" in child psychoanalytic techniques with her own children.

11

Struggles with Libussa

Libussa, unhelpfully, kept Melanie informed all the time she was away with reports of the children's crying and missing their mother.

MUTTI! MUTTI!

SHE HAS EFFECTIVELY SUPPLANTED ME AS HEAD OF THE HOUSEHOLD, AS PARTNER TO ARTHUR AND MOTHER OF MY CHILDREN.

AT THE SAME TIME, IT IS IMPORTANT THAT YOU SHOULD KEEP AWAY FOR THE SAKE OF YOUR OWN HEALTH.

Libussa reported, too, how well the children were developing without their mother. In 1909, Melanie was admitted to a sanatorium in Switzerland for two months.

Libussa and Melanie, lifelong rivals it seems for the men in their lives – first Moriz, then Emanuel and finally Arthur – were inseparable. Arthur realized he had to move out of the social backwater of Silesia and took the family to Budapest.

A YEAR LATER, IN *1911*, LIBUSSA HAD MOVED INTO THE HOUSEHOLD AGAIN, SEEMINGLY PERMANENTLY.

This time, instead of depression, fierce battles ensued between Melanie and Libussa over control of the household and the children. No doubt this period had its toll on the development of the children. Melitta, as if following suit, eventually engaged in bitter public battles with her mother.

The First World War

1914 was a fateful year for Melanie. Not only did the First World War start, but Libussa died a few months after Melanie had her third child, Erich. In addition, Arthur went away to war, a traumatizing experience from which he, and the marriage, never recovered.

Melanie wrote poetry and short stories, and above all she "discovered" psychoanalysis by reading **Interpretation of Dreams** by **Sigmund Freud** (1856–1939) in that year. And she started her own analysis with **Sandor Ferenczi** (1873–1933).

15

Analysis with Ferenczi

At that time, Arthur worked in the same office of a paper mill with Ferenczi's brother, while Emilie's son Otto Pick was Freud's dentist in Vienna. Such links amongst Jewish intellectuals in Vienna and Budapest were common enough. Melanie's analysis with Ferenczi occurred, perhaps intermittently, during the First World War.

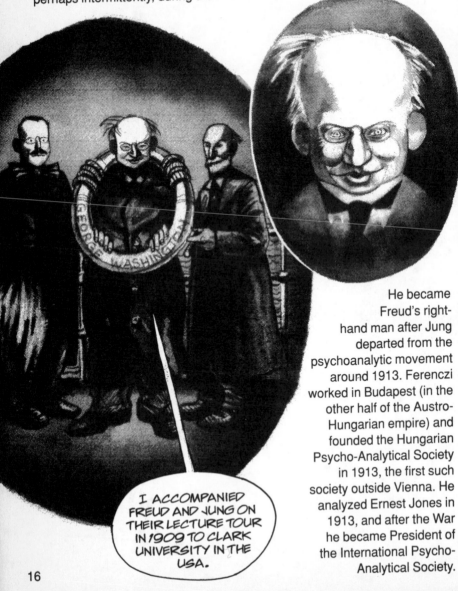

I ACCOMPANIED FREUD AND JUNG ON THEIR LECTURE TOUR IN 1909 TO CLARK UNIVERSITY IN THE USA.

He became Freud's right-hand man after Jung departed from the psychoanalytic movement around 1913. Ferenczi worked in Budapest (in the other half of the Austro-Hungarian empire) and founded the Hungarian Psycho-Analytical Society in 1913, the first such society outside Vienna. He analyzed Ernest Jones in 1913, and after the War he became President of the International Psycho-Analytical Society.

The First World War interrupted psychoanalytic practice, but provided a unique opportunity to develop theories of unconscious processes and the effects of trauma on psychological health. The psychoanalytic understanding and treatment of shell-shock was a long way ahead of any other psychological theory or practice as a way of understanding this form of "war neurosis". And this success dramatically promoted the optimism and growth of the movement.

17

First Encounter with Child Analysis

In those days the relationship between analyst and analysand was very informal, and Ferenczi encouraged Melanie Klein to take an interest in her children psychoanalytically. In that sense, it is probably fortunate for the world of psychoanalysis that she entered into analysis with Ferenczi rather than Freud.

FERENCZI WAS FREE IN HIS THINKING AND ENCOURAGED HIS ANALYSANDS TO DEVELOP AN UNINHIBITED, CREATIVE APPROACH.

I SUPPORTED MELANIE AS A GIFTED, INTELLIGENT WOMAN WHO HAD A SPECIAL INTEREST IN AND TALENT FOR UNDERSTANDING CHILDREN, AND THIS ENABLED HER TO FEEL CONFIDENT IN JOINING AND CONTRIBUTING TO THE MOVEMENT.

CLICK!

Ferenczi had noted Melanie's acute observational skills with children and appointed her clinical assistant, though untrained, to work with him at the Association of Child Research. Thus she moved easily from being a patient to contributing to psychoanalysis itself.

Her drive to be like her father resembled that of Anna Freud, and this may be an influential factor in their later rivalrous battles. In 1919 she gave a paper to the Hungarian Psycho-Analytical Society about child development and schooling that was based on her observations and discussions with her own children. She was admitted as a psychoanalyst on the basis of this paper. By this time, she was also taking her daughter Melitta (then aged fifteen) to meetings of the Society.

Given her frustrated ambition to follow as a doctor in her father's footsteps, perhaps Melanie found a substitute in the world of psychoanalysis.

The Little Hans Case

Analyzing one's own children was a widely adopted method amongst analysts wishing to contribute further to the results of Freud's "Little Hans" case.

LITTLE HANS, A 4½-YEAR-OLD BOY, WAS ANALYZED THROUGH CONVERSATIONS BETWEEN THE CHILD AND HIS FATHER, WHICH THE FATHER THEN REPORTED TO ME FOR MY COMMENTS AND DIRECTION.

5-YEAR-OLD HANS HAD A 'PHOBIA' ABOUT HORSES.

I WON'T GO OUT... A HORSE MIGHT BITE ME!

HIS FATHER CONSULTED FREUD.

IT STARTED WHEN HIS BABY SISTER WAS BORN...

I'M GOING TO HAVE A LITTLE GIRL...

YOU'D LIKE THAT?

YES, NEXT YEAR I'LL HAVE ONE.

WHY SHOULDN'T MUMMY HAVE ONE?

BECAUSE I WANT ONE FOR A CHANGE!

ONLY WOMEN HAVE CHILDREN.

HANS BECAME INTERESTED IN HIS PENIS—AND HIS FATHER'S.

!!

When this "analysis" was taking place in 1908, Freud had just worked out in detail his view of the progress a child makes through various phases – oral, anal and genital – to reach an interim period (a latency phase, setting in around three or four years of age) before adolescence.

IF THE DOCTOR CUTS IT OFF... WHAT'LL YOU WIDDLE WITH?

WITH MY **BOTTOM!**

HANS CONTINUED HIS RESEARCH.

WHAT ARE YOU STARING LIKE THAT FOR?

TO SEE IF YOU'VE GOT A WIDDLER TOO.

DIDN'T YOU KNOW THAT?

I THOUGHT SINCE YOU'RE SO **BIG** YOU'D HAVE ONE LIKE A **HORSE!**

HE HAS DISPLACED HIS FEAR OF **YOU** ON TO HORSES...

WHY SHOULD HE FEAR **ME?**

YOU'RE **BIGGER**... AND YOU MIGHT **THREATEN** CASTRATION BECAUSE HE DESIRES HIS MOTHER.

VERY STRANGE!

PERFECTLY NORMAL PHASE OF INFANCY.

WHAT SHOULD WE DO?

TALK TO HIM... SAY YOU **APPROVE** THAT ONE DAY HE'LL BE AS **BIG** AS YOU.

HOWEVER, THE PHASES WERE WORKED OUT FROM THE PSYCHOANALYSES OF ADULT PATIENTS, EXPLORING BACK BY MEANS OF DREAMS AND FREE ASSOCIATIONS.

Little Hans's conversations were a check on these phases and amply confirmed them for Freud. He then appealed to his co-workers for further information on childhood development from direct observation of actual children.

Early Contributions to Child Analysis

Other analysts eventually did publish similar work on children. It is particularly of interest that Sandor Ferenczi was one of these.

I DESCRIBED A BOY WHOM I LIKENED TO THE PROUD CHARACTER OF CHANTICLEER IN THE CANTERBURY TALES.

And there was a contribution from an important early German analyst, **Karl Abraham** (1877–1925).

I CONDUCTED AN ANALYSIS WITH MY DAUGHTER, HILDA.

AND I LATER ANALYZED MY DAUGHTER ANNA, SUBSEQUENTLY PUBLISHING DISGUISED DETAILS OF THAT ANALYSIS.

I INITIALLY ADOPTED THIS APPROACH—CONVERSATIONS WITH MY OWN CHILDREN—BUT LATER IT WAS CONSIDERED UNETHICAL AND I DISGUISED THE NAMES OF MY CHILDREN IN SUBSEQUENT PAPERS.

All this work confirmed Freud's theories.

Melanie Klein hammered home the main point of her 1919 paper, called "Development of a Child", with great detail. She showed the ubiquitous effect of repression in an inhibited upbringing. For instance, a four-year-old boy (probably her Erich) repeatedly asked, "Where was I before I was born?" or "How is a person made?" Though he fully understood the truthful answer, given in suitable language, that the parents made him, he kept repeating the question.

A CERTAIN PAIN, AN UNWILLINGNESS TO ACCEPT, DETERMINED HIS REPEATED QUESTIONING, EVEN THOUGH A DESIRE FOR THE TRUTH WAS STRUGGLING OUT.

THEN I ASKED OTHERS, MY NURSE OR OLDER BROTHER, WHO TOLD ME THE STORK BROUGHT BABIES.

But, not satisfied, he returned to ask his mother and then seemed more accepting of the truth. He became more talkative and began sorting out truth from stories, such as the Easter hare.

23

The Move to Berlin

Much changed for Melanie Klein in 1921 when the anti-Semitic atmosphere in the new post-war Hungary meant that the family had to leave. Her husband got a job in Sweden.

OUR MARRIAGE HAD BEEN STORMY FOR SOME TIME.

AND MY DEPRESSION, RESTLESS WISH FOR LEARNING AND DESIRE TO TAKE UP A PROFESSION OF MY OWN MADE ME DECIDE TO MOVE TO BERLIN.

The marriage broke up and the end of child-bearing freed Melanie to devote herself to her lifelong intellectual ambitions. The early sacrifice of a profession for family, clearly a tormenting and constantly ambivalent choice, was reversed. Although she was now a divorced mother in an anti-Semitic setting, Melanie was finally able to pursue her ambitions – and did so with great energy and commitment.

24

In Berlin, Melitta began to study medicine – her mother's old ambition. Melanie sought psychoanalysis with Karl Abraham. By this time the whole psychoanalytic movement was becoming more rigorous and professional about the training of new analysts.

ABRAHAM WAS THE MAIN PROTAGONIST OF A FORMAL TRAINING FOR PSYCHOANALYSTS, WHICH INCLUDED A PERSONAL ANALYSIS OF EACH TRAINEE.

And in fact, he set up in Berlin the first Psycho-Analytic Training Institute in 1920. Many foreign students came for this training and were analyzed by Abraham, including Edward and James Glover and Alix Strachey from Britain. 25

The Pioneer, Hermine Hug-Hellmuth

Abraham also encouraged Melanie to treat children, in line with the major growth point in psychoanalytic research in the early 1920s.

Within this atmosphere, her informal method became more standardized into a specific technique. Despite a frosty response when she approached the pioneering **Hermine Hug-Hellmuth** (1871–1924), Melanie's developments were ground-breaking. Hug-Hellmuth was an aristocratic Viennese school-teacher who had made use of Freud's ideas since 1912 by applying them to create a kind of psychoanalytic pedagogy.

I WAS ONE OF THE EARLIEST WOMEN ANALYSTS TO CHALLENGE FREUD'S VIEW OF WOMEN'S PSYCHOLOGY.

I WROTE MY PRINCIPLES OF CHILD ANALYSIS IN 1920: MIXING EDUCATIONAL INSTRUCTION WITH SOME PSYCHOANALYTIC INTERPRETATION.

I RESTRICTED ANALYSIS TO CHILDREN OVER SIX YEARS, AND INTRODUCED A "WARMING-UP" PHASE TO ENGAGE THE CHILD WITH THE ANALYST AT THE BEGINNING OF TREATMENT.

She saw children in their own home and, like Melanie Klein later, she drew attention to children's play rather than the conversational method used with Little Hans. By 1924 she had become the authority on psychoanalytic work with children.

27

Melanie's Work Begins

Melanie Klein undertook her work against the background of belief that children could not be analyzed, especially the very young. She adopted from Hug-Hellmuth an emphasis on play, which became a key treatment tool.

MY APPROACH WAS TO DEVELOP A TRUE PSYCHOANALYSIS OF CHILDREN – USING INTERPRETATIONS AS IN ADULT ANALYSIS –

– RATHER THAN MERELY OBSERVING THEIR PLAY, TALK AND EDUCATION FROM A PSYCHOANALYTICALLY INFORMED PERSPECTIVE.

In consequence, her results tended to do more than merely confirm standard psychoanalytic theories. She was freed to make new discoveries about childhood.

Melanie gave her child patients a set of toys and materials to play with, and a personal locker in which they could keep them. She described this play technique in a later lecture: "On a low table in my analytic room there are laid out a number of small and simple toys – little wooden men and women, carts, carriages, motor-cars, trains, animals, bricks, and houses, as well as paper, scissors and pencils."

EVEN A CHILD THAT IS USUALLY INHIBITED IN ITS PLAY WILL AT LEAST GLANCE AT THE TOYS OR TOUCH THEM.

29

Melanie's attention to rigour impressed people immediately. Alix Strachey, a British trainee in Berlin with Abraham, commented on their first meeting in a letter to her husband.

Melanie Klein's brilliance derives from three things: a realization of the effectiveness of the tool she had developed; then, like Abraham, her possession of an extraordinarily acute ability for clinical observation; and third, a vision of the far-reaching significance of her observations. Her lack of formal medical training was initially an obstacle to her professional development, but it was probably another asset in allowing her to develop her own ideas and thoughts.

Soon, Melanie Klein had all sorts of things she wanted to report.

HOW USEFUL MY SPECIAL TECHNIQUE WAS IN WORKING WITH VERY YOUNG CHILDREN UNDER THREE YEARS OF AGE.

AND I ALSO FOUND THAT I COULD SEE THINGS ABOUT THE DEVELOPMENT OF CHILDREN AT THIS AGE WHICH FREUD AND OTHERS WHO STUCK TO WORKING WITH ADULTS HAD MISSED.

I WENT AGAINST THE PREVAILING ATTITUDE TOWARDS CHILDREN - THAT THEY BE SEEN AND NOT HEARD, AND NOT SEEN TOO OFTEN.

LISTENING TO THEM IN FACT BROUGHT ME SOME STARTLING SCIENTIFIC INSIGHTS.

The Case of Ruth

Melanie made a number of contributions to the topics of the day – the super-ego, the Oedipus complex, and the mysterious development of little girls which male analysts had found rather impenetrable. It is probably no surprise to women that she was able to offer completely new perspectives, but she struggled to be heard in a male-dominated society.

At this time, she stressed her finding of the equivalent in the girl to the boy's castration anxiety. She explained that the girl's fear was connected with the mother's insides.

FOR INSTANCE, RUTH, AGED FOUR, WAS SO HOSTILE THAT SHE WOULD NOT PLAY OR SPEAK TO ME, AND WOULD ONLY STAY IF HER GROWN-UP SISTER REMAINED IN THE ROOM.

After many fruitless sessions, Melanie reported one sequence.

Ruth then astonished Melanie Klein by starting to play with her for the first time.

Differences with Freud . . .

This lessening of the little Ruth's hostility confirmed the accuracy of the interpretation. In general, girls are preoccupied with their hostility to their mother's insides.

THEY FEAR RETALIATION FROM THE MOTHER WHO WILL DESTROY THE CHILD'S BODY, ABOLISH ITS CONTENTS AND TAKE THE CHILDREN OUT OF IT.

This contradicted Freud's view at the time.

CHILDREN DENY THE ANATOMICAL DIFFERENCE BETWEEN MOTHER AND FATHER.

... And Suspicions about Klein

Being a new analyst (and a mere woman), Melanie found it difficult to get her ideas accepted. They were regarded with some suspicion because she was talking explicitly about matters of sex and aggression to very young children.

IN THOSE DAYS, WE WERE OFFICIALLY REGARDED AS PURE AND UNTAINTED AS YET BY THE SEAMY SIDE OF LIFE.

She moved from the role assigned to her as a woman observing children in order to confirm Freud's theories to becoming an original researcher and thinker in her own right.

WOMEN CAN OFFER A NEW PERSPECTIVE ON CHILDREN BECAUSE, UNLIKE MALE ANALYSTS, THEY ARE MORE OPEN TO CONTEMPLATE CHILDREN AS SEPARATE, INTELLIGENT BEINGS.

BUT IT UNSETTLED THE MALE ANALYSTS.

Suspicion that "early analysis" was not a real psychoanalysis, and the continuing affront, in the traditional view, to the innocence of children led to considerable opposition and even ridicule in the Berlin Society.

36

The suspicion was compounded in 1924 when Melanie Klein gave a lecture in Vienna on the new technique and her discoveries. In that year, Hermine Hug-Hellmuth who had pioneered psychoanalytic interventions with children, using her adopted child Rolf, was murdered – by Rolf now grown-up (a fairly strong indicator against analyzing one's own children!).

This occurrence in 1924 a few months before her lecture must have given the Viennese analysts pause for thought, and led to a renewed caution about experimenting with radical new methods on the mental development of children. Melanie Klein was not, however, given to caution when following her own exciting new developments.

The Bloomsbury Set

Melanie's meeting in Berlin at the end of 1924 with **Alix Strachey** (1892–1973) was a fateful one. Alix rapidly became Melanie's admiring friend. Alix was married to **James Strachey** (1887–1967) and both were close to the central figures of the Bloomsbury set in London. Psychoanalysis had a great fascination for the Bloomsbury group – some for it, like Lytton Strachey (James's brother) and Maynard Keynes; others against it – such as Clive Bell and Roger Fry.

When Leonard and Virginia Woolf set up their publishing house – The Hogarth Press – they were persuaded by James Strachey to become Freud's English publisher. James and Alix emerged as his official translators and editors.

Alix Strachey found Melanie Klein vivacious and even entertainingly outrageous and reported this in a letter to her husband.

Melanie was just the sort of character the Bloomsbury set wished to cultivate: intelligent, outspoken and challenging the male-dominated view of society.

Through Alix's contacts in London, the British Psycho-Analytical Society invited Melanie Klein to lecture there. A series of six lectures were arranged in 1925, and these were a great success. On her return to Berlin, Melanie found that Karl Abraham had fallen ill. He died on Christmas Day, 1925. The effect of another bereavement must have been profound, and it paved the way for another move.

Acceptance in Britain

Ernest Jones invited Melanie Klein to move to London in 1926. He was the great organizer of psycho-analysis world-wide. Born in South Wales in 1879 (died 1957), loyal disciple and later biographer of Freud, he was already the elder statesman of psychoanalysis in Britain.

THE REASON FOR THE INVITATION WAS THAT JONES HAD ME IN MIND TO ANALYZE HIS OWN CHILDREN.

Mervyn Jones, then three years old, and his sister Gwynneth aged five started being analyzed immediately after Melanie's arrival in September. Jones's wife Katherine also started analysis with Melanie a month later. 43

The Climate for Analysis in London

Melanie's own children joined her in London shortly afterwards. She was rapidly acclaimed as the most original investigator within the London group of psychoanalysts. Already there had been an interest in child analysis. Mina Searl had begun analyzing children in 1920. Mary Chadwick, Susan Isaacs and Ella Freeman Sharpe were also developing child analysis as a speciality in London. The British Society had a strong suffragette contingent of women who were actively seeking professional standing in the period of radical social change after the war.

MiNa SEarL

ELLa fReeMan SharPE

Psychoanalysis was a new profession open to women, whilst the traditional professions of law and medicine remained closed. Many ex-teachers joined the British Psycho-Analytical Society soon after its founding in 1919, perhaps because of an interest spawned in the strong current of reform and progressiveness in British education at the beginning of the century. **Susan Isaacs** (1885–1948) established the first experimental school on psychoanalytic lines. **Donald Winnicott** (1896–1971), a paediatrician, was already training as a psychoanalyst in 1924.

mary chadwick*

DONALd WiNNicoTt

SuSAN isaacs

Melanie Klein found herself not only welcomed by the Jones family but arrived happily in a psychoanalytic culture, ready for experiment, seeking its own emerging identity and committed to child analysis. Automatically, with her talents and the draw of her personality, she moved immediately to the centre of British psychoanalysis.

FOR A DECADE, I EXPANDED MY WORK WITH CHILDREN, BUILT UP A LARGE PRACTICE, AND PRODUCED A NEW PAPER NEARLY EVERY YEAR...

...WHICH REPORTED ON PROGRESS IN MY THEORIES OF CHILD DEVELOPMENT.

Origin of Klein's Object-relations

The use of the toys, many of them small male or female figures, clearly pointed towards the relationships with, and between, **objects**. She put less emphasis on Freud's focus upon the tensions caused by sexual energy (libido). He had described the instinct as having a *source*, an *aim* and an *object*.

OF THESE THREE, MY LIBIDO THEORY THREW ATTENTION UPON THE **SOURCES** (EROGENOUS ZONES) AND THE **AIM** (ITS DISCHARGE).

The object was somewhat incidental, and is in any case very variable because human instincts are plastic and change remarkably from one object to another. In contrast, Melanie Klein emphasized the object; and in particular, after Karl Abraham, she stressed the anxieties about (and for) the people and things which the child related to. Other object-relations psychoanalysts – for example, the earliest Scottish analyst **Ronald Fairbairn** (1889–1964) and his follower **Harry Guntrip** (1901–75) – have dispensed with the notion of instinct altogether to concentrate on the relationships with object.

I NEVER WENT SO FAR AS THIS, AND RETAINED THE NOTION OF AN INSTINCT WITH A MATERIAL SOURCE WITHIN THE BODY.

Her work founded the "object-relations" school of psychoanalysis, a feature of British psychoanalysis ever since. She was naturally drawn in this direction by her use of toys, through which children clearly displayed objects (people) in relation to each other.

THIS PLAY WITH "OBJECTS" - THE TOYS - SHOWED THE CHILD'S UNCONSCIOUS PHANTASIES BECOMING ACTIVE IN ITS MIND.

Children were remarkably responsive to being taken seriously in this way. If she was correct in what the play meant, this would bring relief to the child.

I WAS STRENGTHENED IN THE BELIEF THAT I WAS WORKING ON THE RIGHT LINES BY OBSERVING THE ALLEVIATION OF ANXIETY AGAIN AND AGAIN PRODUCED BY MY INTERPRETATIONS.

Children's worries are not realistic ones as a grown-up would see them. But they have a logic of their own, connected to the kind of truth that Freud had discovered in dreams.

The Case of Peter

Melanie thought a consistent *unconscious* content threaded its way through the anxious play. So, as she talked to the child about its play, she would relate it to what she thought were the deeper (unconscious) meanings in the child's mind.

Her interpretations begin simply. For instance, the case of Peter, described in one of her London lectures in 1926.

PETER WAS THREE YEARS OLD AND VERY DIFFICULT TO MANAGE, CLINGING STRONGLY. HE COULD NOT TOLERATE FRUSTRATION, AND WAS TOTALLY INHIBITED IN PLAY.

52

THIS INNOCENT AND "ORDINARY" PLAY WAS BORING AND UNIMAGINATIVE. I ASKED HIM WHAT THE CARRIAGES WERE DOING.

THAT'S NOT NICE.

HE STOPPED BUMPING THEM TOGETHER AT ONCE, BEING INHIBITED AT THAT PRECISE POINT.

THIS INHIBITION, UNDER MY VERY NOSE, APPEARS TO BE CONNECTED WITH HIS FEELING THAT SOMETHING IS "NOT NICE" - SO HE'S STOPPED PLAYING.

So, because something or other is "not nice", therefore he becomes inhibited. But already the play seems to indicate some actual cause of inhibition represented by carriages bumping together, and quite possibly that is an *unconscious* meaning.

Then, once again, Peter started knocking the two toy horses together in the same way, upon which she said:

Ideas about the horses dying and then burying them indicate more imagination, less inhibition. And that change occurred after her comment that the horses were *people*. Klein was interested in that sort of change – the freeing up of inhibition.

In his second session, Peter arranged the cars and carts in the same two ways as before – in a long file and side by side. At the same time, he once again knocked two carriages together, and then two engines – just as in the first session.

NEXT HE PUT TWO SWINGS SIDE BY SIDE AND SHOWED THE INNER AND LONGISH PART THAT HUNG DOWN AND SWUNG.

LOOK HOW IT DANGLES AND BUMPS.

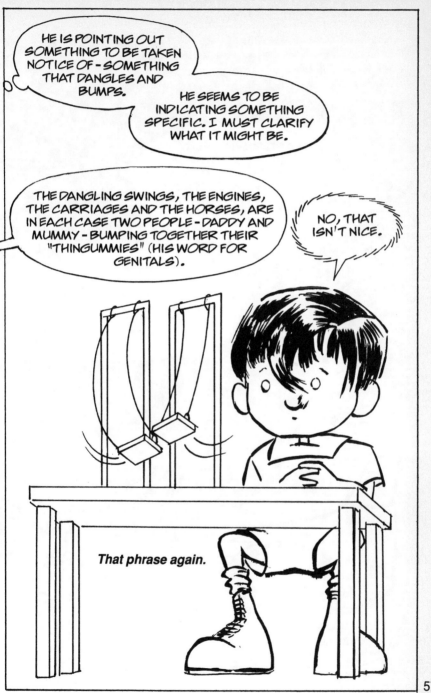

It is difficult not to conclude that Melanie Klein's interpretation really does connect with something that worries Peter; something to do with his parents together, something in fact very troubling which they do with their genitals – and which is "not nice" for him. Immediately, Peter spoke about his little brother again.

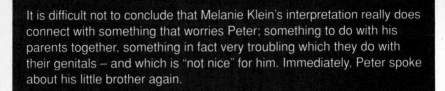

THIS PATTERN – HIS PLAY AND THEN HIS CONCERN ABOUT HIS BROTHER – OCCURRED IN THE FIRST SESSION. IT POINTS TO A SIGNIFICANT LINK BETWEEN HIS INHIBITION AND HIS BROTHER. SO . . .

YOU THOUGHT TO YOURSELF THAT DADDY AND MUMMY BUMPED THEIR THINGUMMIES TOGETHER AND THAT IS HOW YOUR LITTLE BROTHER FRITZ CAME.

So, Peter is preoccupied with the arrival of his brother; it troubles him – a "not nice" activity.

Peter's response to that interpretation was striking. He changed to a quite different play, describing various toys by name, including his hated brother, and a fantasy about chickens being let out.

HE BECAME A CHILD IMAGINATIVELY GETTING UP TO ALL SORTS OF THINGS WITH A VARIETY OF DIFFERENT KINDS OF RELATIONS GOING ON BETWEEN THE FIGURES IN A MUCH RICHER SEQUENCE.

Melanie Klein repeatedly showed that this development from inhibition to a much more imaginative play is the effect of making simple but quite explicit interpretations of the child's worries.

Disputes Begin

Anna Freud (1895–1982) started her career as a school-teacher, but following her own psychoanalysis she commenced in her father's profession in 1923. Perhaps because she was analyzed by Freud, she was involved in a lifelong devotion to him.

IN THAT YEAR, 1923, MY FATHER WAS DIAGNOSED AS HAVING THE CANCER FROM WHICH HE EVENTUALLY DIED.

HER LOYALTY TO ME DURING MY LONG ILLNESS MAKES HER MY IDEAL SUCCESSOR.

This was an invitation that Anna loyally accepted. She led an unhappy and strikingly cloistered life, absorbed in consolidating her father's work. Perhaps it was important both to her and her father that they make an "official" contribution to the contemporary growth-point of psychoanalysis, child analysis.

The first step was to teach a course on child analysis in 1925 at the Vienna Institute of Psycho-Analysis, and she published the lectures a year later.

The extreme caution of Anna Freud's approach led her to begin her lectures by contrasting her view with Melanie Klein's sweeping claims to be able to treat all disturbances in children.

THE MAJORITY OF OUR MEMBERS THINK DIFFERENTLY . . .

ONLY CASES OF INFANTILE NEUROSIS CAN BE TREATED, AND ONLY THEN IF THE CHILD ACTUALLY SUFFERED, INSTEAD OF THE REST OF THE FAMILY.

To get conscious agreement required a period of "breaking the child in" for analysis. The requirement of conscious cooperation went along with her verbal technique. Though observing that play might be useful, she argued against Melanie Klein's specific interpretation of the child's play as equivalent to free association of ideas in adults.

PLAY DOES NOT HAVE THE SAME PURPOSE FOR A CHILD AS THE ADULT'S WORDS. IT CANNOT SERIOUSLY APPROACH THOSE PRE-VERBAL STAGES THAT ARE POSSIBLE IN ADULT ANALYSES THROUGH FREE ASSOCIATION.

The Problem of Transference

Anna Freud claimed too that "Because the child is still deeply related to the actual parents, it does not form transferences to the analyst." These attempts to engage the patient, together with the fatalism about the transference, led to combining educative methods with psychoanalytic exploration into a more didactic technique. She, as Freud, worked on the basis that the power of a psychoanalysis was the strength of positive feelings the patient transferred towards the person of the psychoanalyst. Love for the analyst overcame the resistance to the pain of becoming aware of the unconscious.

Transference was the term Freud used, because it appeared to be a love transferred from another relationship (with a parent) at an earlier developmental period. Anna thought transference could not occur in children.

A CHILD OF THREE, SAY, IS NOT YET OUT OF THE PERIOD OF ORIGINAL LOVE ON WHICH TRANSFERENCE WILL EVENTUALLY BE BASED. SO IT CANNOT TRANSFER THIS LOVE.

Anna believed that in child analysis the psychoanalyst had to cultivate a sufficiently positive attitude from *realistic* (not transference) sources. She recommended that this loving had to be won in a preparatory or "warming-up" phase.

All through her lectures, Anna explicitly or implicitly argued against Melanie Klein's view that full analytic interpretations could be made, just as in adult analyses. The vehemence of Anna's criticism also resulted from her anxiety about being so explicit with children.

The British analysts held a symposium in 1927 about Anna Freud's criticisms and published their papers.

OUR CHARGE AGAINST ANNA FREUD IS THAT SHE HESITATES TO PROBE THE DEPTHS OF THE UNCONSCIOUS.

Joan Rivière

AND ALL THE MEANS WHICH WE WOULD REGARD AS INCORRECT IN ADULT ANALYSIS ARE STRESSED BY ANNA FREUD WITH CHILDREN.

Melanie described difficult children with whom she could work, even though they started with negative transference feelings. She showed that Anna Freud's warming up phase was not needed, provided that interpretations were "deep" enough.

63

Totemic Fathers

One unfortunate implication which this symposium conveyed was that Anna watered down analysis for children.

BECAUSE HER OWN ANALYSIS HAS NOT ADEQUATELY DEALT WITH HER RESISTANCES, AND PARTICULARLY, HER OEDIPUS COMPLEX WAS NOT RESOLVED.

This led to a correspondence between a very uncomfortable Jones and an angry Freud who had conducted his daughter's analysis. Freud got personal.

Jones' letter

ANNA CERTAINLY WAS ANALYZED FOR A LONGER TIME AND MORE PROFOUNDLY THAN YOU!

Melanie strove to develop her work from a basis of Freud's ideas, whereas Anna's efforts were to adhere to her father's ideas precisely, without change. Both were caught in the struggle to be great daughters for their respective fathers, but Melanie was able to develop in a creative way.

WOULD THINGS HAVE BEEN DIFFERENT IF I HAD BEEN FREUD'S DAUGHTER?

One must have sympathy for Anna who had a far "greater" father to live up to, and one who survived longer than Melanie's, who died when she was eighteen. One could speculate about Melanie's switch to psychoanalysis – and whether she would have done so had her father survived beyond her twenties.

Refining Freud's Theories

In the end, British analysts prevented Anna Freud's book from being published in English for some twenty years. In contrast, Melanie Klein's important book, **The Psycho-Analysis of Children**, was published in 1932. It contained a development of her London lectures and brought her acclaim from nearly every one of her colleagues in Britain. And greater than ever suspicion from analysts in Europe.

Melanie Klein put faith in her technique because she could draw significant new conclusions about the development of children. The responses to her explicit interpretations did confirm the psychoanalytic theories of the Oedipus complex, but her observations did more. They could refine the details of that theory.

SOMETIMES THESE THEORIES WERE PUZZLING FOR THE MALE ESTABLISHMENT TO COUNTENANCE.

NOT ONLY WERE CHILDREN ACTIVE, THINKING BEINGS, BUT GIRLS HAD DIFFERENT PHANTASIES FROM BOYS – ONES IT NEEDED WOMEN ANALYSTS TO UNCOVER.

She challenged standard theories in other ways, claiming that the Oedipus complex did not start with the genital phase (age three onwards) but earlier; and that the super-ego is not the outcome of the Oedipus complex but precedes it.

67

Tackling Psychotic Disorders: the Case of Dick

Ambitiously, Melanie began to tackle the puzzle for psychoanalysis of the major psychiatric disorders – schizophrenia and manic-depressive psychosis. In schizophrenia particularly gross disturbances of symbolization occur. This is evident in the case of four-year-old Dick, who might now be diagnosed as autistic, and who started in analysis in 1929. His development had been arrested at the level of a baby of eighteen months.

HE UTTERED MEANINGLESS SOUNDS, OCCASIONALLY USED A FEW WORDS INCORRECTLY, AND DID NOT SEEM TO WISH TO BE UNDERSTOOD.

THERE WAS NO PLAY, AND HE RAN ABOUT THE CONSULTING ROOM AIMLESSLY.

The only interest he displayed in life was in trains and stations and in doors and their handles. These were the only rudimentary symbols in his play.

However, at the first psychoanalytic session, Dick began to show a response to interpretations, which convinced Klein that a true symbolic world – and life – could be enhanced by psychoanalytic understanding. When she produced the toys for him to play with, he looked at them without the slightest interest. To engage him, she picked out the train which she knew was the one interesting toy for him.

I PUT A BIG ONE BESIDE A SMALLER ONE AND HAZARDED A PSYCHOANALYTIC GUESS.

I CALLED THEM "DADDY TRAIN" AND "DICK TRAIN".

At that, he picked up the "Dick" train and rolled it towards the window.

STATION.

THE STATION IS MUMMY. DICK IS GOING INTO MUMMY.

Whereupon he left the train and ran into the space between the outer and inner door to the room, where it was dark, shut himself in and said "dark".

DARK.

The idea of objects getting into a dark and empty inside space seemed to link his obsessions with trains and doors. As he repeatedly ran in and out of the dark space between the doors, Melanie said . . .

IT IS DARK INSIDE MUMMY. DICK IS INSIDE DARK MUMMY.

NURSE?

Whilst she was saying this, he asked "Nurse?" She reassured him that nurse was coming soon – which he repeated back to her correctly.

In this sequence, the indifference at the beginning, and the play with the train, moved a little towards a degree of actual relatedness to the analyst about his anxiety over his nurse.

IN SUBSEQUENT SESSIONS THIS ANXIETY BECAME MUCH MORE EVIDENT.

Melanie Klein thought that this slight progress towards being able to express his worries — even to feel those worries — showed the power of her method. Dick's analysis continued (with an interruption during the War) for nearly twenty years, but he was eventually able to lead a normal enough life.

An Empty Space

In the same year that she started with Dick, 1929, she was struck by a biographical account of a woman who suffered fits of depression.

This woman had a highly-tuned artistic sensibility, though she had never painted. One day a picture of an important artist was removed from a wall in her home, leaving a gap which yawned emptily – and suddenly represented the gap inside her.

It brought on a kind of familiar and apathetic sadness. But with some encouragement from her husband, she spent a day with paints, daubing the wall until exhausted. When her husband returned, he found with astonishment a masterly creation on the wall. In fact, she subsequently did paint and exhibit and received acclaim as an artist.

THE POINT IS THAT AN INTERNAL EMPTINESS CAN BE IN SOME WAY FILLED WITH SYMBOLIC ACTIVITY.

Filling the Space with Symbols

Dick's actual retreat into dark empty spaces, and this proto-artist's obsession with the empty gap on the wall, were at this time important to Melanie Klein. They linked up with her earlier ideas of girls' phantasies about the space inside – where babies exist – and which becomes a battleground.

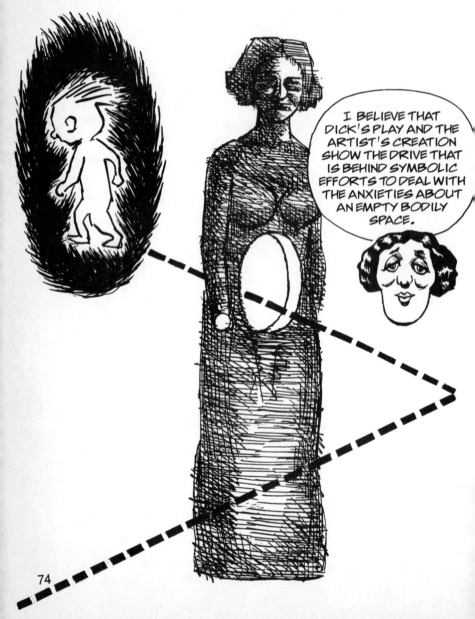

I BELIEVE THAT DICK'S PLAY AND THE ARTIST'S CREATION SHOW THE DRIVE THAT IS BEHIND SYMBOLIC EFFORTS TO DEAL WITH THE ANXIETIES ABOUT AN EMPTY BODILY SPACE.

In another case at this time, John, aged seven, had learning difficulties. Typically he mistook the French words "*poulet*", "*poisson*" and "*glace*". After Melanie enabled him to produce his associations in words and drawings to the three things – "chicken", "fish" and "ice" – he had a dream. The fish was a crab and John was standing on a pier where he often went with his mother. He had to kill an enormous crab which came out of the water.

But when John had done so, more and more crabs came out of the water. He had to kill each of them because they would kill the whole world. Most of all, the crabs wanted to get into something in the water, like both a house and a joint of meat.

THE MEAT OR HOUSE IS MOTHER'S BODY, AND IS BEING ATTACKED BY A DANGEROUS DADDY -

- THE CRABS REPRESENT FATHER'S THREATENING PENIS -

- AND MANY OF THEM.

This interpretation gained the child's cooperation.

This sort of clinical material shows the interference with learning and the use of symbols (the French words), which come from anxieties about very primitive and psychoanalytically understood phantasies. Though John was not as disturbed as Dick, development was stunted by anxieties about spaces and gaps. They are gaps which, it seemed, in the course of development can be filled by symbols, if anxiety about them is not too great.

This extremely intricate understanding of patients' phantasies, symbols and development led to increasing interest in psychotic patients. But in addition, it made Melanie Klein a leader in the adventurous exploration of the most primitive layers of the mind. Intrigued, many younger psychiatrists wanted to have their own analysis with her.

Clifford Scott came from Canada to seek out Melanie Klein. Paula Heimann and Herbert Rosenfeld came when they left Germany. There were English analysts too – Joan Riviere, Donald Winnicott, Susan Isaacs, Roger Money-Kyrle and many others – who were now intrigued by her striking and intricately illustrated developments.

Paula Heimann

Roger Money-Kyrle

Herbert Rosenfeld

By this time, she was regularly conducting psychoanalyses of adults. Adrian Stokes, an important art critic, was one of them, drawn by her work on symbolism and aesthetic creativity.

One of the most intriguing followers was Melitta, Melanie's eldest child, one of the first to be analyzed by Klein when she was a child. Indeed, Melitta was quite a disturbed woman, and it has been suggested that she too suffered from a psychotic disorder.

susan isaacs

donald winnicott

clifford scott

Joan Riviere

Melanie Klein had taken the lead as the foremost clinical investigator in the British Psycho-Analytical Society. However, psychoanalysis in Europe was about to undergo a devastating collapse as Nazi Germany overran the continent and swept away this "Jewish science".

As her opponents in Europe were being severely threatened, Melanie Klein's achievements reached their height. In 1935, she made her first major contribution to theory which began to distinguish a distinctly Kleinian perspective. This step came to be called the "**depressive position**".

The Depressive Position

Melanie used the term "depressive position" out of respect for Freud and her own analyst Karl Abraham, who had been forerunners in this work.

THEY HAD BOTH BEEN INTERESTED IN THE PSYCHIATRIC CONDITION OF *DEPRESSION* AND HOW IT SEEMED TO REPRESENT A STATE OF AFFAIRS IN WHICH ORDINARY MOURNING HAD GONE WRONG.

MOURNING TAKES PLACE WITH A SLOW SEVERING OF THE LINKS WITH A LOST PERSON.

Memories are taken out one-by-one, as it were, and each one requires "psychic work" to repeat the knowledge that the person is gone – just as old letters, clothes and belongings of the loved one have to be relinquished.

THAT INTERNAL, MENTAL WORK TAKES A LONG TIME, BUT EVENTUALLY NEW OBJECTS AND INTERESTS WILL BE FOUND. THE PERSON WILL GO OUT TO THEM CAUTIOUSLY BUT WITH INCREASING FREEDOM FROM THE PAST.

Mourning and Melancholia

However, Freud said things can go wrong. The person may get stuck and be unable to go out to a new object.

> THIS WILL OCCUR WHEN THERE HAS BEEN AN UNUSUAL AMOUNT OF AGGRESSION TOWARDS THE LOVED ONE.

> IN THAT CASE, THE DEAD PERSON IS "TAKEN INSIDE" THE EGO, AND THE SUBJECT IN SOME IMPORTANT SENSE *BECOMES* THE LOST PERSON.

When this happens, the ego then receives the aggression and punishment that the object once received. This is the state of severe self-punitive depression, known to Freud as **melancholia**.

The Fate of the Lost Object

This concentration on the fate of the object – to be given up or to be internalized – is an example of a move away from the strict lines of the libido theory. It opened the way to specific theories of object-relations. Karl Abraham then developed this idea, emphasizing the concern about the object's fate.

I ESTABLISHED THAT IT WAS NORMAL FOR THE LOST OBJECT TO BE RESTORED INSIDE THE PERSON – KEPT ALIVE THERE.

THIS CAN OCCUR WHEN THERE IS NOT THE DEGREE OF AGGRESSION THAT I TALKED OF IN MELANCHOLIA.

It is not surprising that Melanie took an interest in mourning and in depression. She herself had several bouts of depression, often connected with her significant losses. In 1914, by the age of thirty-two, Melanie had lost her sister, father, brother and mother. Her analyst died suddenly in 1925 whilst treating her. And her son Hans died tragically in a climbing accident in 1934 that many believe was a suicide. It is more than likely that her own experience of depression deeply affected her ability to mother her children. Indeed, it was due to depression that she was away for eighteen months when Melitta was still a baby.

Loss and Creativity

One could speculate that Melanie's decision to pursue her psychoanalytic career and research was reinforced as a way of dealing with the emptiness of devastating loss.

We can only admire her resilience in being able to convert these terrible experiences into an opportunity for creative development, whilst recognizing that her own insight played an enormous part in the development of her ideas.

Klein's Idea of Position

Melanie Klein introduced the idea of a "position". She used this to mean the position in relation to an object – a position has characteristic anxieties, defences and phantasies. The term often gives perplexity.

THE TERM "PHASE" IS NOT REALLY SATISFACTORY, BECAUSE I AM NOT TRYING TO REPLACE THE PHASES THAT FREUD HAS DESCRIBED – ORAL, ANAL, GENITAL AND SO FORTH.

ORAL
ANAL
GENITAL

Indeed, it would have been injudicious at that time to discard anything of Freud.

AFTER ALL, THAT IS WHAT JUNG HAS DONE.

Understanding the Depressive Position

Melanie thought she was describing a genuinely different level of the mind – of the unconscious. There were in fact the phases of the libido as Freud had described, and the specific anxieties that attached to each of those, but these were the neurotic level of human experience.

ORAL
ANAL
GENITAL

PSYCHOTIC ANXIETY

BEHIND THESE (OR RATHER, BENEATH THEM), LIES A DIFFERENT AREA OF THE MIND WHICH IS DOMINATED BY WHAT I CALL "PSYCHOTIC ANXIETY".

This is more primitive, more infantile. If Freud had discovered the child in the adult, then Klein believed she had discovered the infant in the child.

These underlying anxieties don't go away at a later stage, they are simply dealt with in different ways at different levels of the mind.

AS THE BABY MATURES INTO THE CHILD, NEUROTIC MECHANISMS COME TO THE FORE AND OVERSHADOW THE "PSYCHOTIC" ONES, ALTHOUGH THESE NEVER DISAPPEAR.

She was at pains to illustrate carefully and exhaustively what she meant, and we must follow this, intricate though it is.

89

What Does Klein Mean by "Psychotic"?

One consequence is that people thought Melanie Klein was saying that babies were "psychotic". She did not mean this. "Psychotic" meant that the anxieties which exist in all of us are the origins of particular difficulties in some people – those who eventually choose an abnormal developmental route for one reason or another and become psychiatrically ill. It was unfortunate to pick a psychiatric diagnosis as a term for ordinary processes.

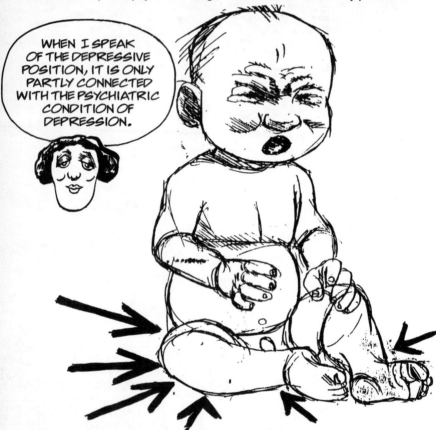

WHEN I SPEAK OF THE DEPRESSIVE POSITION, IT IS ONLY PARTLY CONNECTED WITH THE PSYCHIATRIC CONDITION OF DEPRESSION.

She believed that the form of anxiety that is at the core of the depressive position – called depressive anxiety – can, in some people, drive them mad – manic-depressive. But not in others who are pushed forward to the more usual phases of development.

Depression itself can be thought of as a state which arises when the depressive position does not work out properly, when conflicts are not adequately resolved and severe pressures remain unconsciously at the root of someone's personality.

The depressive position usually becomes a normal enough state of mind, although a rather painful one, like mourning. Melanie Klein tried once to introduce the much more vivid term "pining" to cover the ordinary experience, but it did not catch on. She did not think that the goal of life was happiness – or pleasure as Freud put it.

INSTEAD, I ACKNOWLEDGE OTHER IMPORTANT SATISFACTIONS, INCLUDING THE SATISFACTION OF STRIVING TO *RESOLVE CONFLICTS*.

So, What is the Depressive Position?

Let us return to Karl Abraham again. He noticed how disturbed patients, manic-depressives, can become preoccupied with taking things inside themselves, typically by eating them. This may occur in dreams or in phantasies – or even in the psychotic patient actually eating a variety of bizarre objects, including faeces, which represent something lost!

ONE OF MY PATIENTS HAD BECOME ENGAGED TO A YOUNG WOMAN.

LATER, HE BEGAN TO REJECT HER IN HIS FEELINGS.

AT WHICH POINT, HE SUCCUMBED TO A DEPRESSIVE AND DELUSIONAL CONDITION.

As he recovered, a *rapprochement* occurred with his *fiancée*. There was then a further relapse and rejection of her. During this time he had a symptom – clenching his anus. This seemed to be a bodily "holding fast" to the contents of the bowel, and this represented an attempt to retain inside himself an object which once again he was about to lose.

A few days later, he told his analyst that another symptom had taken the place of the first.

As Abraham remarked: "We have here a confirmation of the theory that at the deepest levels the loss of an object is an anal process and its introjection an oral one."

Taking Inside Oneself: Introjection

Freud developed this idea and described how the loved one, now inside the person, becomes a part of their actual identity – how they see themselves.

THEY BELIEVE THEY ACTUALLY DISPLAY CHARACTERISTICS OF THE PERSON THAT HAS BEEN TAKEN INSIDE.

I MYSELF, WHEN MY FATHER DIED, NOTICED THAT MY OWN HAIR WAS NOW GREY.

His actual perception of himself had been radically re-adjusted by his bereavement, so that he came to resemble for himself a feature of the father he had lost.

Timing the Super-Ego

Freud's idea was that normal development involved giving up the parents as sexual objects around the age of three or four years. The child did this by internalizing those parents. Thereafter, they became a real part of the personality of the child, his "super-ego", and watched over him from inside, as it were.

AT FIRST, I CALLED THIS IDENTIFICATION.

I CALLED IT INTROJECTION.

Melanie Klein developed Freud's notion in a strikingly different, though perplexing, way.

MY WORK WITH VERY YOUNG CHILDREN, BEFORE THE AGE THAT FREUD WAS TALKING ABOUT, SHOWED SOMETHING QUITE EXTRAORDINARY. CHILDREN SEEMED TO BE OCCUPIED WITH A SUPER-EGO LONG BEFORE THE TIME FREUD ASSIGNED.

She placed this internalization very early indeed, long before the genital phase at three years.

95

Working From the Inner State

Melanie, close to her many experiences of bereavement and depression, could perhaps think creatively about it. This work could be seen as a very personal attempt to resolve her own depression, as well as her sensitivity to the difficulties of her own children who had undoubtedly suffered from her absences, either during her travels or depressions. Her paper, "A Contribution to the Psychogenesis of Manic-Depressive States", was read in August 1934 to the International Congress of Psycho-Analysis at Lucerne, four months after the death of her son Hans. Just as Freud's most fundamental work, **The Interpretation of Dreams**, came out of his own self-analysis, so it seems Melanie Klein's great original contribution came from her own efforts to overcome and make sense of her bereavements and her inner state.

Internal Objects

Melanie Klein's particular conception of the internal world was extraordinarily profound, yet perplexing. She had discovered a very rich life with introjected figures. It is as if children play with these figures inside themselves, in much the same way as they play with toys, anxiously but inventively to reassure themselves.

I WAS ABLE TO ASCERTAIN THAT THIS INTERNAL WORLD OF OBJECTS PERSISTS IN ADULTS, QUITE EXPLICITLY IN DISTURBED PATIENTS, BUT AT VERY DEEP LAYERS OF THE UNCONSCIOUS IN ALL OF US.

The depressive position represents a concern for these internal objects – and is thus a significant development beyond Abraham and Freud, who described the relations with external objects, albeit often in very bodily terms. What does the idea of an "internal object" mean? This was a question on everyone's lips in the Psycho-Analytical Society after 1934. 97

A Case Example of Internal Objects

One of Melanie Klein's adult patients complained about his different physical troubles. He described what medicines he had taken – enumerating what he had done for his chest, his throat, his nose, his ears, his intestines, etc. It was as if he were nursing these parts of his body and his organs.

I AM ALSO CONCERNED ABOUT THE YOUNG PEOPLE UNDER MY CARE (I AM A TEACHER). AND I AM WORRIED ABOUT SOME MEMBERS OF MY FAMILY.

THIS ATTITUDE OF CONCERN FOR HIS INSIDE OBJECTS (HIS ORGANS) IS MIRRORED IN HIS CONCERNED RELATIONS FOR EXTERNAL OBJECTS (PUPILS AND RELATIVES).

He appeared to relate to those internal organs as he would to actual people, except that they were inside him. He associated the different organs he was trying to cure with his internalized brothers and sisters.
He worried about them, feeling guilty, and he had perpetually to keep them alive.

This sense of internal figures is strongly conveyed through the link with similar external ones that he loves – his family.

THE INTERNAL OBJECTS (ORGANS AND PARTS OF HIS BODY), EXPERIENCED VERY CONCRETELY AS ACTUAL LITTLE PEOPLE INSIDE HIM, ARE LOOKED AFTER PHYSICALLY, LIKE ILL MEMBERS OF HIS FAMILY.

This experience is not a conscious one, and in fact remains remote from consciousness. Odd though it is to experience live objects inside, we do sometimes in everyday idiom talk of butterflies in the stomach or a frog in the throat. It is not uncommon for people to have some conscious concern or caring relationship with parts of their body that are actually diseased or damaged. One might say "my poor foot" if it has been bruised and hurt – rather than "poor me". Internal objects have this quality of "otherness" (or rather others who belong).

Another Case Example: Unconscious Phantasy

Another adult patient experienced alien beings inside himself in the form of intestinal worms.

WHEN I WAS TEN YEARS OLD, I FELT I HAD A LITTLE MAN INSIDE MY STOMACH WHO CONTROLLED ME AND GAVE ME ORDERS WHICH I HAD TO OBEY.

I HAD SIMILAR FEELINGS ABOUT MY REAL FATHER'S REQUESTS OF ME.

THE WORMS EXPERIENCED IN ADULTHOOD ARE AN ALTERNATIVE EXPRESSION OF SOMETHING SIMILARLY BAD INSIDE HIM – WHICH COULD BE CALLED AN "INTERNAL FATHER".

This kind of play activity inside the person is known as "unconscious phantasy". And these phantasies are often very violent and aggressive. They are different from ordinary day-dreams, or "fantasies" (spelled 100 with an "f").

Initially, Melanie Klein had been quite alarmed by the degree of aggression she found in her little patients. So many children seemed to play without joy and to be anxiously intent on dealing with awful, violent situations. She called these states a "paranoid position". But when she realized that these represented aggression *inside*, she could understand what very severe insecurity the child felt for itself, as well as for these internal objects.

One profoundly important phantasy was the child's attempts to deal inside itself with its violence towards its parents. We saw three-year-old Peter killing horses, which represented his mother and father with their "thingummies", and burying them.

THE INTERNAL PARENTS WHO HAD INTERCOURSE WERE A PARTICULAR PROVOCATION AND GAVE RISE TO SPECIALLY VIOLENT PHANTASIES – AND THERE-FORE TO PARTICULARLY DISASTROUS INTERNAL STATES.

The Combined Parent Figure

The active internal mother and father are called the "combined parent figure". This idea of parents in intercourse is closely connected with Freud's description of the Oedipus complex. It does, however, have very primitive aspects and may have little to do with the actual parents – and it is, astonishingly, occurring as a drama in some internal space.

THIS PHANTASY OF COMBINED PARENTS IS THE EARLY VERSION OF THE OEDIPUS COMPLEX.

Only later, it evolves into Freud's classical view of the Oedipal relations with the actual parents at a different and more mature level of the mind.

Because the child also loves his parents, his concerns reach a peak over the realization of his hatred of them. Violence towards them escalates as he experiences them in intercourse together *inside* him. This massive insecurity about the internal state, the concerns to control the violence and the anxiety about the loved parents, form a crisis for the very young child.

This crisis is called the depressive position.

Particularly anguishing is the confluence of love and hatred – the violence on the one hand, and the emerging concern on the other – resulting in a devastating internal state for the child. The primitive quality of these phantasies, which comprise "depressive anxiety", suggest a very early origin in children's development – actually during the first year of life, Melanie Klein calculated.

Externalizing the Internal

Because he is concerned about his loved parents, the child makes heroic efforts to deal with the situation. One device the child resorts to is trying to work out this situation in terms of external objects. He externalizes, or "projects" the internal objects (the figures of his parents) into the external world. Or in other words, he sees the objects actually in the figures of his parents. And a great deal of his own phantasy is then lived out through them.

IF THE CHILD FEELS HIS VIOLENCE HAS ACTUALLY HARMED HIS PARENTS, HE MAY ACTUALLY SEE THEM AS WEAK AND DAMAGED.

IF HE SEES THEM AS UNDAMAGED OR RETALIATORY AGAINST HIS OWN VIOLENCE, HE WILL SEE HIS ACTUAL PARENTS AS POTENTIALLY THREATENING AND DANGEROUS...

...AN EXTERNAL SITUATION WHICH IS THEN CATASTROPHIC.

But, out there, the danger may be more easily avoided; or there may be other helping objects that might be recruited to assist.

Reparation

One of the most important reactions the child has to these violent phantasies is to attempt to repair damage he has done. Melanie Klein regarded a process of "reparation" as a major element in the development of the child. An example is that of the artist who "filled in" the gap where the missing picture had been (see pages 72–4).

REPARATION IS THE SOURCE OF A VERY GREAT MANY ACTIVITIES IN LIFE AND FORMS A CORE OF THE IMPULSE TOWARDS CREATIVITY.

In these instances, the reparation is towards external objects as representatives of those inside that are damaged. They are external objects that once restored can be internalized as repaired internal ones. 105

Reparation is an attempt to mobilize positive loving feelings to dominate over hatred, and thus to rescue the parents in whatever surviving condition.

Often the child will use its early and emerging erotic feelings to enhance its love, giving rise to a precocious sexuality, or an enduring erotic pattern of behaviour at times of crisis.

The internal object establishes the core of the personality. If there is a conviction that the important object inside is a *bad* one, this will lead to anxiety about the internal state and a long-standing emotional or mental disturbance – like the man who thought he had worms inside him (see page 100).

The Good Object Inside: Richard's Response

However, the child may introject a *good* object. That is to say, he feels inside him an object that is benign, one which loves and wishes to protect, help and support him. It provides a deep internal sense of well-being.

One example is ten-year-old Richard. On one occasion, Melanie Klein had cancelled a session. At the next one, Richard met Mrs Klein on the way to the playroom and was delighted that she had the key. It appeared to him that the cancelled session yesterday had meant that the playroom might never again be available.

Melanie reminded him of a previous occasion when a session had been cancelled and he had dreamed of a deserted car. He had switched the electric fire on and off (as if coming alive and dying) to express a fear of Mrs Klein and his Mummy dying. Richard stopped playing with the toys and looked straight at her, and he answered quietly and with deep conviction.

THERE IS ONE THING I KNOW, AND THAT IS THAT YOU WILL BE A LIFELONG FRIEND OF MINE.

He added that Mrs Klein was very kind, and that she was doing him good, though it was sometimes unpleasant. He could not say how he knew it was doing him good, but he felt it.

Richard's moving response demonstrated how a deep sense of internal well-being had returned to him. He had acquired it as a part of himself so that it might become a lifelong friend. His subsequent play was happier, lively and inventive. The presence of internal objects, like Richard's, creates a profoundly important basis for the relationship with the self. In that instance, it is a benign one.

Identification with internal objects is ever-changing, and depends in part on the enormous influence of the actual external object, its behaviour, presence or absence.

Coming to Terms with Reality

One crucial aspect of the external object is its capacity to understand the child, and particularly (even paradoxically) to understand its very worst feelings. And, contrary to general assumptions, adults and parents who can refer calmly to death and damaged objects can have the effect of reviving hope and making the patient feel more alive. Though perhaps he is alive and sad, he is not alone with his worries.

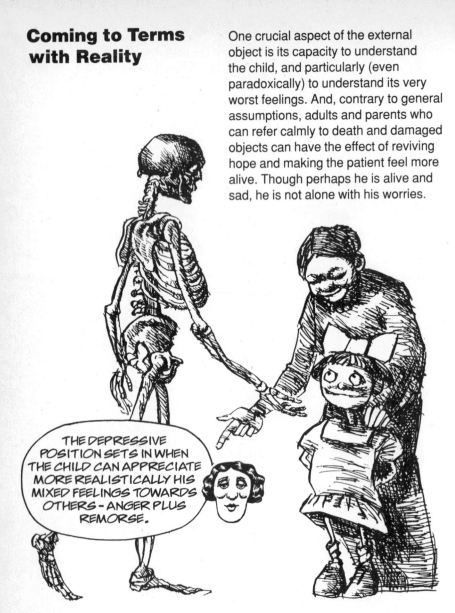

THE DEPRESSIVE POSITION SETS IN WHEN THE CHILD CAN APPRECIATE MORE REALISTICALLY HIS MIXED FEELINGS TOWARDS OTHERS – ANGER PLUS REMORSE.

Melanie Klein argued that the success of this step into concern and mixed feelings depends heavily upon the process of internalizing a good loving object that produces a sufficient state of well-being.

If the good internal object is felt to be securely possessed, as Richard did (for all time, he thought), it gives a strong support and confidence when the person is under stress.

As the infant begins to feel *for* the object, he becomes less egocentric. But at this point he is at risk. He is prone to fears that he will damage this loved object whenever his frustration and anger are high. The reality of external objects can then be very important.

His hatred and anger have then been transformed by his love into concern and remorse, with some possibility of repairing them.
When he can feel more reassured that his objects can survive his crises of violence, then he can allow the external ones more separateness. He needs to control them less, and omnipotence declines.

The Pain of the Depressive Position

Concern and sadness, typical of the depressive position, are profoundly painful human emotions. Melanie Klein speaks of "pining" for a loved object that has suffered or been lost. The intensity of pain over the unexpected death of her son Hans was at its height as she wrote her paper in 1934. And it did not go quickly. A second paper read to the Psycho-Analytical Society in October 1938, "Mourning and its Relation to Manic-Depressive States", was written as a further attempt to clarify the depressive position for her colleagues, many of whom found her descriptions of the internal world obscure. But it is likely that it was also part of her long working-through of this bereavement. It records in detail the bereavement of a mother who has lost a son – almost certainly herself. The state of mind and the dreams of the bereaved mother are also linked back to the death of a brother when she was twenty (Melanie's admired Emanuel).

Persecutory Guilt

Frequently, the pain of the depressive position is just too severe. Melanie described this as a kind of persecutory guilt that ensures punishment – never forgiveness. In this situation, the person may enter a manic state. That state is a form of defence against pining. It is relieved by a refusal to feel need.

THE LOST PERSON IS INSIGNIFICANT. SO THEREFORE THERE'S NO SERIOUS LOSS!

THIS STATE OF MIND IS A TRIUMPH OVER BEING DEPENDENT OR IN NEED, ESPECIALLY AN EMOTIONAL NEED. SUCH A STATE IS A REMNANT OF EARLY "OMNIPOTENCE".

AN ALTERNATIVE RETREAT FROM THE GUILT, WHEN IT CANNOT BE TOLERATED, IS TO ENTER A PARANOID STATE OF MIND.

This demonstrates how painful the sadness and pining can be – if even persecution is preferred! Melanie had found that experiences of terror and violence were alarmingly common in the children she analyzed. She had originally called this the "paranoid position".

113

Projection and Introjection

When a child suffers *pavor nocturnus* (night terrors), Melanie thought that it was beset by the panicky belief that something very evil was about to attack the child, especially from inside. Temper tantrums represent a development of this terror, in the sense that the fearful enemy to be fought is now outside the child. Through a process of "projection", he may then transfer the cause of aggression from inside the self to outside. The persecutory feelings of guilt, dealt with by projection, create a protesting wounded or dead external figure that threatens and persecutes.

We saw with Richard how something very benign can be moved from outside to inside. In that case, the good analyst who is not dead became a benign internal state of well-being. That is called "introjection".

Now, in complementary fashion, something dangerous that is felt to be inside can be moved outside – a process of "projection". It can then be treated as an evil accuser unreasonably demanding condemnation and punishment – exacting its pound of flesh. It is then avoided, as in phobias, or made insignificant and itself guilty, as in many forms of criminality. The pain, re-established as persecution from outside, can be dealt with by counter-accusations.

115

Trouble in the Psycho-Analytical Society

At the time of her bereavement in 1934, Melanie Klein began to suffer the beginning of a prolonged series of attacks on herself and her work. She was no stranger to being criticized for her achievements. But these had hitherto come from analysts on the continent – in Berlin when she had been there, and subsequently from Anna Freud in Vienna. But from 1934 onwards, a hostility within the British Psycho-Analytical Society gathered.

That hostility was led at first by her daughter Melitta – now Melitta Schmideberg after her marriage. "Analyzed" as a child by Melanie Klein herself, she later had two other analysts. She began with yet a third, **Edward Glover** (1888–1972), a close colleague of Ernest Jones and one of the most senior members of the British Society.

Glover was scientific secretary of the British Society, and later of the International Psycho-Analytical Association. He, together with his new analysand, Melitta, turned hostile attacks upon Melanie. Psycho-analytical Society meetings were frequently disrupted by Melitta's heckling of her mother.

KLEINIANS USED TRAINING, SCIENTIFIC MEETINGS AND EVEN THE ANALYSES THEY CONDUCTED FOR PARTISAN PURPOSES.

She and Glover were different. "After we abandoned scientific discussions as a poor way of dealing with zealots, we joined in the power politics."

One can only imagine the intense embarrassment these crusading attacks must have caused Melanie, who had striven to promote her daughter's career, as she had her own. One must question the behaviour of Glover, as Melitta's analyst, joining in a conspiracy with Melitta to discredit Melanie's work. The history of psychoanalysis is sprinkled with examples of the dangers of analyzing close relatives or acquaintances. However, within a psychoanalytic confraternity, it is impossible not to know one's analyst – and one's analysands – in other contexts.

Melanie Klein's independence of mind had forged ahead during the 1930s. In contrast, the psychoanalysts on the continent of Europe, mostly German-speaking, were engaged in consolidating the progress already made over half a century. However, consolidation was not to be. Psychoanalysis was virtually wiped out in Europe by the Nazi invasions. The Freud family escaped to London in 1938 – to re-establish classical psychoanalysis there.

Melanie Klein had some deep misgivings about giving shelter to Freud, his family and their colleagues from Vienna. She believed it endangered her own work.

Freud himself died in 1939. The exiled Viennese, led by his daughter Anna, fought even harder to consolidate his work. A massive struggle ensued to sustain the unique quality of British psychoanalysis, on one hand, and on the other to consolidate the classical approach. Anna Freud, grateful for being rescued by the British after the Nazi take-over of Austria, was uncomfortable about the heat of disagreement.

However, neither woman was prepared to consider compromise. Both sides felt they had everything to lose. One is left to wonder about the influence of their fathers on these equally stubborn daughters.

A Three-Way Split

The outcome was an agreement to a stalemate, and the British Psycho-Analytical Society divided into several sets of followers – eventually three societies in one. Anna Freud did not recover the allegiance of the British analysts for Freud's classical psychoanalysis. She kept her group of Viennese *émigrés* around her and attracted a steady group of students (including Joe and Ann-Marie Sandler) and immense support from the USA where, without a medical degree, she could not have practised if she had settled.

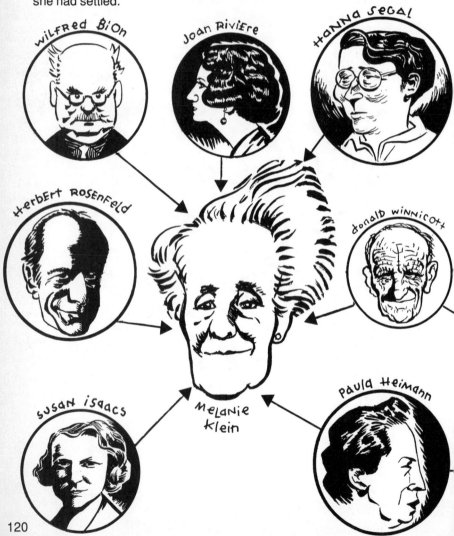

wilfred Bion

Joan Riviere

Hanna Segal

Herbert Rosenfeld

donald Winnicott

susan isaacs

Melanie Klein

paula Heimann

Melanie Klein did not retain the whole-hearted support she had once had from the British analysts. Instead, her following was reduced only to Joan Riviere, Paula Heimann and Susan Isaacs – and some trainees, Herbert Rosenfeld, Hanna Segal and Wilfred Bion. In between, as a kind of buffer zone, were the British group who came to be known as "Independents" – Sylvia Payne, Marjorie Brierley, Ronald Fairbairn and Ella Freeman Sharpe, and eventually Donald Winnicott and Paula Heimann, who moved away from the Kleinian group. Some new refugees, notably Michael Balint and Michael Foulkes, became prominent Independents. Ultimately, three separately angled trainings arose, and each of these groups developed theory and practice in its own way.

AnNA FreuD

ann-MaRIE Sandler

JOE SandleR

donald WiNNiCott

SylviD PaYNE

MaRJORIE bRieRleY

PAULA heimann

RoNaLd faitbaith

Ella FreeMan · ShArPe

MICHAEl balint

Klein's Interest in Psychotic Conditions

Perhaps because of this three-way diversity, Melanie Klein was driven to more original and adventurous developments yet. But hints and indications of her later discoveries lie within her earlier work – especially her interest in the severe disorders of manic-depressive illness and schizophrenia. She had treated a number of psychotic children. Some trainees with medical and psychiatric trainings – Clifford Scott and Herbert Rosenfeld – began to work in psychiatric hospitals in Britain. Her supervision of their work, and with one or two schizophrenic patients of her own, led Melanie Klein to broaden her interest from manic-depressive conditions to schizophrenic ones. She sought explanation of their very strange internal world, to which she had already been alerted.

Clifford Scott

Herbert Rosen

Part-Objects

This work pointed to the primitive defence mechanisms of "splitting". In one process of this type – "splitting of the object" – the person sees its objects in a form which magnifies one feature to such proportions that it eclipses all others in the personality. Bad objects are experienced as *all* bad – simply intent on destroying the child. Good ones are, in contrast, *all* good, with solely a benign interest in doing good for the child.

BECAUSE EVERYTHING IN LIFE IS MIXED, THESE PRIMITIVE STATES TEND TO DECONSTRUCT OBJECTS INTO "GOOD" AND "BAD" BITS (CALLED "PART-OBJECTS").

The Bad Breast

One simple example is a baby who is hungry and feels hunger pains in his stomach. Because he has not yet got mastery of his faculties, what does he believe?

When mother eventually comes to feed him, he may not see her as someone to get comfort from, but instead as an opportunity to project his "bad" internal object into. He can't feed then because his mother's breast is now an angry, gnawing, deadly thing with a solely evil intent against him.

SOME BABIES ARE PARTICULARLY PRONE TO TURNING AWAY FROM THE BREAST WHEN THEY ARE MOST IN NEED OF ITS COMFORT – AS IF IT IS A DANGEROUS PREDATOR.

SOMETHING BAD IS GNAWING AT ME FROM INSIDE!

Splitting the Ego

In a related process of splitting, the person divides his own self. This is called "splitting of the ego". Some aspect of the self is separated and obliterated, as if it were not a part of the personality at all. Often people will deny all knowledge of aggression in themselves. Or, as in those recidivist criminals mentioned above (see page 115), all guilt is separated off and abolished from their personalities.

Projective Identification

In this process of "splitting the ego", additional support may be gained from projection or introjection – but particularly the former. In that case, the person does not believe himself to be aggressive; rather, he believes that he is wholly harmless, and some other person is picked out as the aggressive one.

In this case, the projector may become somewhat depleted and rendered limp in character, as he loses part of his personality.

The loss of parts of the identity through finding them in another person is called "projective identification". These primitive processes are usually driven by the need to defend against aggression.

Narcissism

And these defence processes have very profound and extraordinary effects on personal identity. The export of aggression enhances the sense of benignity of the person – but through a fear of threat from outside. The import (introjection) of good objects equally leads to the sense of an internal goodness in the person.

If these powerful and primitive mechanisms seriously disturb the picture of the real person, then this is considered "narcissism".

This is a different way of describing the state that Freud called narcissism in which only the self exists and there is no significant object at all.

127

Freud's theory of **narcissism** was based on the way in which the **libido** is directed. Libido, as the mental energy that is expressed as attention, interest and excitement, is first directed at the self – as if other people or objects did not exist.

THIS IS THE STATE OF MIND OF THE INFANT AT BIRTH AND FOR SOME PERIOD AFTER IT.

Only later does the libido "turn outward" towards other objects: the baby can then recognize and evaluate others in its actual surroundings.

Melanie Klein's view is instead thoroughly rooted in object-relations. There is no "object-less" state at birth. That is to say, narcissism results from the interchange – in phantasy – with an object, so that good qualities of all kinds reside within the self, and all bad in the object.

HOWEVER, IT IS NOT JUST QUANTITIES OF GOODNESS AND BADNESS THAT ARE EXCHANGED ACROSS THE BOUNDARY OF THE SELF, BUT ACTUAL ASPECTS OF PERSONALITY AS WELL.

Attitudes, functions, mannerisms, taste, moral standards and a host of other things may be acquired from the parents or others. The whole character is deeply influenced and formed by the removal from it of unwanted, noxious characteristics – together with the accumulation within the personality of qualities (usually) felt to be good. The reverse of this process and the creation of a more realistic view of oneself constitutes the development of character.

Klein's View of Healthy Development

Development of character involves a capacity to acknowledge the bad aspects of the self as well as the good ones.

One consequence of a balanced development is integrity and strength of character.

To support a one-sided characterization of the self as good, even mental functions may be split off, Klein believed. For example, she described criminal activity in children and concluded that the criminal (even as adult) loses his morality in order to evade a sense of guilt.

For a schizophrenic, it is his own capacity to think which he splits up. In that way he avoids knowledge of a painful and maybe dangerous world that he perceives around him. Such a person is deeply unrealistic.

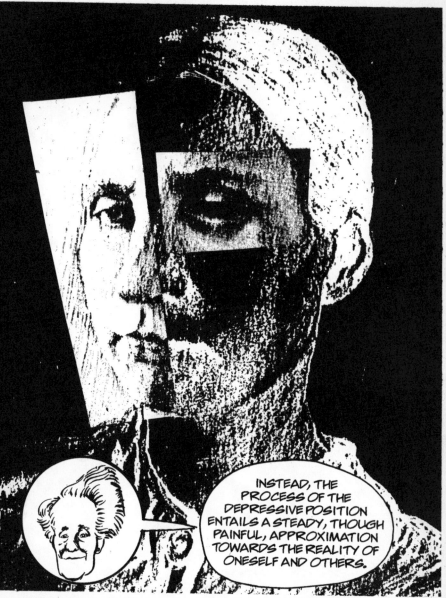

INSTEAD, THE PROCESS OF THE DEPRESSIVE POSITION ENTAILS A STEADY, THOUGH PAINFUL, APPROXIMATION TOWARDS THE REALITY OF ONESELF AND OTHERS.

Objects become less one-sided exaggerations. And the self has to be acknowledged equally as some mixture of good and bad qualities.

The Paranoid-Schizoid Position . . .

The split-up state is not the depressive position. In 1946, Melanie Klein began a full-scale investigation of what she now called the "paranoid-schizoid position". People who become schizophrenic, she believed, went down a blind alley developmentally in the very early stages after birth. That period is dominated by a set of experiences of extreme fear and insecurity, as if there were a profound belief in some evil agency (a bad object) that intends to cause harm or death.

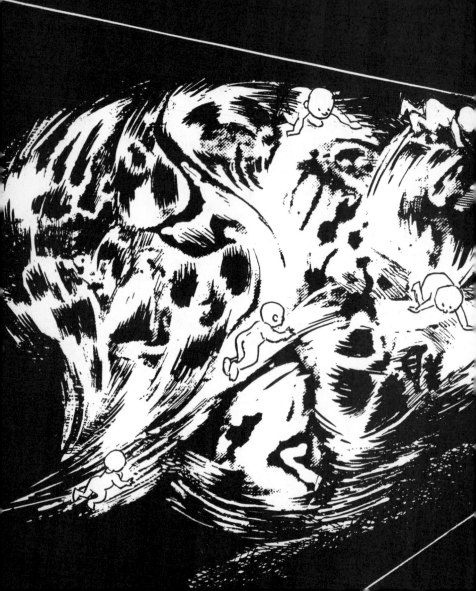

. . . and the Death Instinct

THIS IS A VERY EARLY STATE IN WHICH THE BABY EMPLOYS PRIMITIVE DEFENCE-MECHANISMS TO ALLAY THE TERRORS OF THE EARLIEST ANXIETIES.

These, she believed, resulted from the effects of the **death instinct**, a hypothetical construct that Freud had postulated, and which Melanie Klein thought she found as a real phenomenon in the clinical material of terrified children and of schizophrenic patients.

The basis on which people develop their conscious feelings is unclear, but it seemed plausible to Melanie Klein and her small group that there is a bed-rock of early experiences that are given, as it were, and do not have to be learned from experience. For instance, the capacity to feel hunger, we might accept, is there from birth. And so indeed is the suckling reflex. A newborn infant will turn towards a finger tickling its cheek and suck it. This reflex represents the outward mechanical response which corresponds to an inward **experience** of an expectation that there will be something comforting to suck.

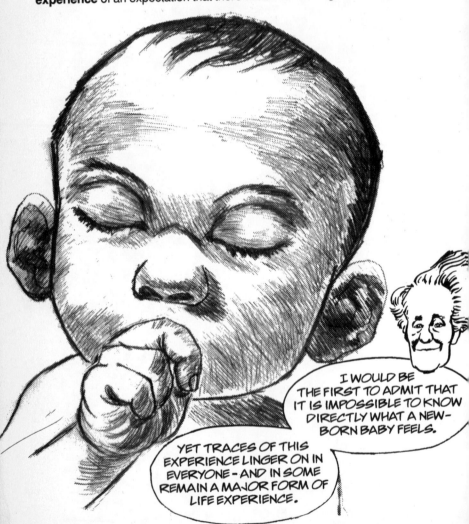

I WOULD BE THE FIRST TO ADMIT THAT IT IS IMPOSSIBLE TO KNOW DIRECTLY WHAT A NEW-BORN BABY FEELS.

YET TRACES OF THIS EXPERIENCE LINGER ON IN EVERYONE – AND IN SOME REMAIN A MAJOR FORM OF LIFE EXPERIENCE.

One inherent premonition is some extreme terror that we later come to call "death".

Preconceptions

One of Melanie Klein's students, **Wilfred Bion** (1897–1979), who became perhaps the foremost of her followers, explored the philosophical implications of many Kleinian concepts.

He called this innate expectation (the early premonition, for instance, of death) a "preconception". It is the propensity to have an experience when the baby meets the right external conditions.

SUCH AN INNATE PRECONCEPTION – OF, SAY, A NIPPLE – IS FORMED IN THE BIOLOGY AND EXISTS BEFORE THE FIRST DISCOVERY OF ONE.

IT THEN MEETS THE REALITY, A REAL NIPPLE.

AND THIS FORMS A CONCEPTION – "THE NIPPLE" – WHICH BECOMES A MENTAL OR PSYCHOLOGICAL ENTITY.

At the same time, that development, according to Bion, creates the pressure for a mental apparatus to think these thoughts or conceptions.

The Fear of Death From Within

Some preconceptions relate to expectations of the self. In this vein, Melanie Klein thought there was an innate propensity to feel the terror of death. This becomes realized under certain circumstances – neglect, pain, prolonged hunger, etc. Moreover, she described a particular content to the experience. It had a specific phantasy, like the specific phantasies she discovered in children's play.

THE FEAR OF DEATH TAKES THE FORM OF A BELIEF THAT SOMETHING INSIDE THE PERSON IS SEEKING TO PULL HIM APART AND RENDER HIM DEAD BY DISMEMBERMENT.

This is a more profound fear than that of merely losing the sexual member (castration anxiety) described by Freud.

Persecutory Anxiety

The core anxiety of psychotic patients is the fear of a self-inflicted damage from within. The crucial aspect is "from within". Previously, Klein had described the fear of attack from other external objects – or even internal objects – which she had originally called the paranoid position.

Then she described the fear of damage to, or death of, the internal loved object (linked so often to the external one) which she called the **depressive position**.

NOW I AM DESCRIBING A PRIMITIVE *SELF*-DESTRUCTIVENESS. THIS IS A SECOND "PSYCHOTIC ANXIETY" TO PUT BESIDE DEPRESSIVE ANXIETY.

She found this self-destructiveness occurring in disturbed patients and called it "persecutory anxiety". Defences against this anxiety, which she had already described (splitting, projection, introjection), she now called schizoid mechanisms. And this whole state of mind she called the **paranoid-schizoid position**.

137

Klein described a curious patient who did not feel things which he, and others, might have expected him to feel. Instead he felt – and seemed – flat and empty. The patient actually experienced one part of himself as lost or annihilated.

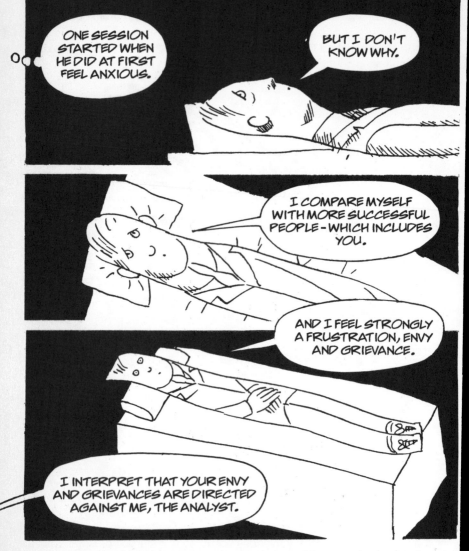

At that precise point, his mood changed abruptly. His tone of voice became flat and expressionless; and he said that he felt detached. Though the interpretation seemed correct, it no longer seemed to matter to him. He had no wishes any more. Nothing was worth bothering about.

Melanie Klein points to this dramatic moment at which his feelings literally went missing. Something quite specific had disappeared from his personality. She explained it as a strong and destructive defence.

THE PATIENT SPLIT OFF THOSE SPECIFIC PARTS OF HIMSELF WHICH HE FELT TO BE DANGEROUS AND HOSTILE TOWARDS THE ANALYST.

HE TURNED HIS DESTRUCTIVE IMPULSES ONTO HIMSELF.

Unconsciously, in his phantasy, this blankness amounted to an annihilation of part of his personality.

The characteristic anxiety felt in these states is the fear for one's own integrity. Klein argued from such clinical material that the patient's unconscious phantasy is that he, in reality, inflicted a debilitating wound on his own mind. She likened this to Freud's study of the Judge Schreber case. Schreber had invented a delusional "world system" during a period of acute paranoia which he reported in an autobiography that Freud analyzed in 1911.

I FEEL THE WHOLE WORLD HAS BEEN ANNIHILATED IN A "WORLD-CATASTROPHE".

THIS IS A PROJECTION OF SCHREBER'S FEELING THAT HIS EGO WAS SPLIT. IT IS THE ANNIHILATION BY ONE PART OF THE SELF OF THE OTHERS, WHICH IS A SCHIZOID MECHANISM.

Melanie Klein's students were able to repeat these observations on hospitalized schizophrenics. Most notable among the students were **Hanna Segal**, who wrote important introductory books on Melanie Klein's ideas, and **Herbert Rosenfeld** (1909–86), whose schizophrenic patient 140 we will now meet.

A Projective Form of Identification

One fundamental observation that the group of Kleinians began to make, was reported by Melanie Klein as a "projective form of identification". An example is a chronic schizophrenic man analyzed by Herbert Rosenfeld. The patient's mind was severely damaged and could not sustain thought or communicate meaning. One Saturday he assaulted the nursing Sister, attacking her suddenly while having tea with her and his father. He hit her hard on the temple when she affectionately put her arms around his shoulders.

On Monday and Tuesday he was silent. On Wednesday, a little more talkative. He said he had destroyed the whole world and then added one word.

And then he said "Eli" (God) several times. He looked very dejected and his head drooped on his chest.

The apathetic, disjointed and fragmented communication of the chronic schizophrenic expresses the state he feels his mind is in, literally destroyed of all meaning.

The analyst then interpreted as follows.

WHEN THE PATIENT ATTACKED THE SISTER, HE FELT HE HAD DESTROYED THE WHOLE WORLD AND HE FELT ONLY ELI, OR GOD, COULD PUT IT RIGHT.

HE FELT NOT ONLY GUILTY BUT AFRAID OF BEING ATTACKED INSIDE AND OUTSIDE.

The patient became more communicative, saying "I can't stand it any more". It was a strikingly understandable emotional response – despair. But he then returned to his disabling form of communication. Staring at the table, he said . . .

IT'S ALL BROADENED OUT, WHAT ARE ALL THE MEN GOING TO FEEL?

The analyst attempted to give all that a meaning too – that the patient could not stand the guilt and anxiety inside himself and had put them into the outer world so that he felt broadened out, split up into many men, and then wondered what all the different parts of himself were going to feel, now outside him.

The meaning which this interpretation hazards depends upon understanding how splitting and projection occurs in schizophrenic patients. In this instance, the persecuting guilt over the attack on the nurse was dealt with desperately by turning a fragmenting aggression against the self. Then those fragments are spread out into many other objects in the external world (projective identification).

The response to that interpretation was more explicit, although still not fully couched in verbal symbols.

He then looked at a finger of his which was bent and said . . .

I CAN'T DO ANY MORE, I CAN'T DO IT ALL.

As before, the response is direct and clear, filled with feeling; and it makes contact with the analyst and with us.

It suggests that the reconstructed meaning has brought some more appropriate understandable state back to the patient – from wherever it has been. The patient then pointed to one of the analyst's fingers which was also slightly bent.

A part of the patient (his bent finger) was linked to a part of the analyst (who also has a bent finger). This is the kind of evidence which the Kleinians took as confirmation that something of the patient is discovered in an external object, *in* the analyst in this moment – i.e. in his bent finger.

The phantasy that parts of the patient are projected and actually located in an external object is termed "projective identification". It is a remarkably concrete phantasy, as much so as the phantasy of internal objects. These phantasies are so real for the patient that the spreading of his mind abroad *does* deplete him and make him actually incoherent as his world of meaning fragments and disperses.

Previously we came across a similar process that Melanie Klein had described in criminals (see page 115).

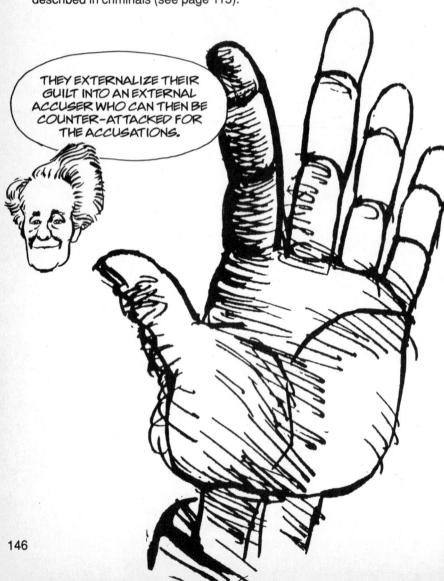

THEY EXTERNALIZE THEIR GUILT INTO AN EXTERNAL ACCUSER WHO CAN THEN BE COUNTER-ATTACKED FOR THE ACCUSATIONS.

It was only when Klein could discuss with her students their severe hospitalized schizophrenics that she could formalize precisely the paranoid-schizoid position and projective identification. This she did in a paper in 1946 called "Notes on Some Schizoid Mechanisms".

THIS NEW THEORY HAS MORE OR LESS SEALED THE TRIPARTITE STRUCTURE OF THE SOCIETY, SINCE FEW APART FROM MY CLOSE GROUP AND THE STUDENTS I SUPERVISE CAN GRASP THESE ADVANCED IDEAS.

For the next three decades, and long after her death, the practice of Kleinian psychoanalysts and child analysts was deeply moulded by the very concrete notion of split off parts of the mind located in others.

147

Transference

As with many psychoanalytic concepts, what was discovered in disturbed patients was subsequently found occurring in significant traces in most people. The concepts of "splitting" and "projective identification" proved enormously fertile and have led to clarification of all sorts of phenomena. For one thing, the psychoanalyst can understand transference much more precisely.

This pictures the transference differently – no longer an essentially past moment, repetitiously recreated. Instead, it is conceived as a here-and-now process using the object for the purpose of a projective identification. It supports the splitting of the patient's ego.

In these terms, the patient uses the present objects in primitive ways. This position *vis-à-vis* the object – using it in a particular way – is appropriate at much earlier stages in development.

Alongside this new vision of transference as an active process in the present, a new conception of counter-transference suddenly grew up around 1950 in many analysts' thinking.

149

Counter-Transference

Counter-transference had originally meant the troublesome side of the analyst which reacted unconsciously, and problematically, to the patient's transference. Now it could be seen that the analyst's reaction to the transference could represent an accurate reception of a projection from the patient.

WHAT THE ANALYST INTROJECTS COULD, UPON REFLECTION, REVEAL THE PROCESSES THE PATIENT WAS ENGAGED ON WITH HIS OBJECT, THE ANALYST.

COUNTER-TRANSFERENCE WAS THUS REVERSED FROM BEING AN INTERFERENCE TO BECOMING A POTENTIAL SOURCE OF VITAL CONFIRMATION.

This reversal of fortune for the concept of counter-transference was highly controversial.

Melanie Klein disapproved on the grounds that poorly analyzed psycho-analysts could excuse their own emotional difficulties – blaming their patients in effect for what *they* feel. This led her into direct conflict in the mid-1950s with one of her group, Paula Heimann, who had been most loyal to Melanie Klein during all the difficult times of the preceding ten years. A sad rift between these two began then and was never healed.

In fact, the trend within the Kleinian group was to take seriously the new view of counter-transference, especially amongst the younger members, Wilfred Bion and Roger Money-Kyrle. They examined the phenomena from both the analyst's troubled experience and the patient's informative projections. Bion described this as a "containing function". The analyst is required to "contain" projects of the patient's intolerable experiences, as a mother must "contain" the alarm injected into her by her screaming child.

IN A SIMILAR WAY, THE ANALYST IS RECRUITED TO PERFORM THE FUNCTIONS OF A MOTHER TOWARD A NEW-BORN BABY.

Bion thought of this in terms of a mother who actually does have to feel the baby's alarm and terror when it cries. Sometimes a mother can carry this tension that arises in the baby, and sometimes she is put into her own panic. So too the analyst, said Bion.

Repetition and the Death Instinct

Melanie Klein's work with children had grounded her whole development. In her observations, she found the most extreme manifestations of aggression and fear. Because of this, she was the most respectful of analysts towards Freud's peculiar notion of the death instinct.

Freud had made a study of *repetition*, in the sense of a repeated experience of traumatic pain. Repetition could occur either in the mind as dreams, or in transference, and maybe within certain group phenomena; or as actually repeating in some form the trauma itself.

THIS SHOWS EVIDENCE OF A DEEPLY PERVERSE STREAK IN HUMAN NATURE THAT AIMS TOWARDS PAIN, UNPLEASURE AND ULTIMATELY DEATH.

He thought of this as a general biological (even cosmological) principle.

It astonished Freud that soldiers who had been traumatized by shell-shock in the First World War continually *relived* the trauma in dreams and in daytime flashbacks. This "repetition-compulsion" contravened his principle that the mind operates to reduce tension and pain. In these instances, pain and death were apparently invited by reliving them.

I CALL THIS THE "DEATH INSTINCT". BUT I DO NOT BELIEVE THAT IT IS DIRECTLY OBSERVABLE IN THE PSYCHOANALYTIC SETTING. IT IS "CLINICALLY" SILENT.

Freud considered that there was no way in which the method of psycho-analysis as it then was in 1920 could reveal an impulse to self-destruct. Self-destruction was behind the compulsion to repeat, but this could not be verified by the practical methods largely resting upon symbol-interpretation and dream analysis.

Following the revolution in the understanding of transference (and counter-transference), to which the notion of projective identification contributed enormously, a number of Kleinian analysts have sought to show that the death instinct is not clinically silent.

The death instinct reveals itself clinically in the subtle interactions of the splitting and the unconscious transference and counter-transference relationship between patient and analyst.

155

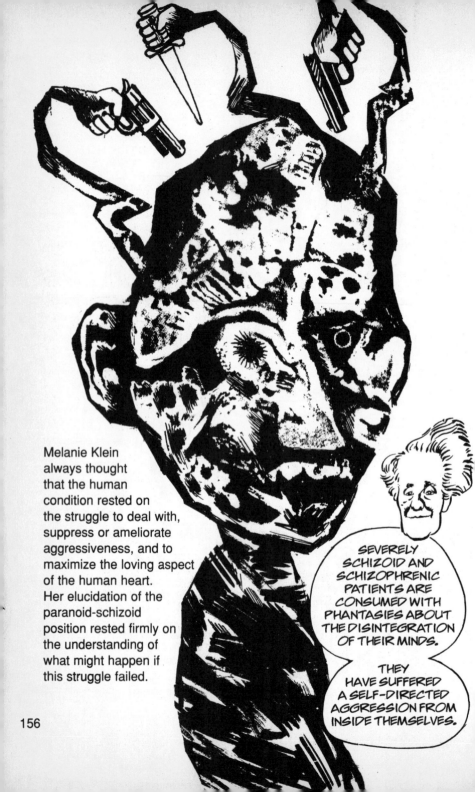

Melanie Klein always thought that the human condition rested on the struggle to deal with, suppress or ameliorate aggressiveness, and to maximize the loving aspect of the human heart. Her elucidation of the paranoid-schizoid position rested firmly on the understanding of what might happen if this struggle failed.

SEVERELY SCHIZOID AND SCHIZOPHRENIC PATIENTS ARE CONSUMED WITH PHANTASIES ABOUT THE DISINTEGRATION OF THEIR MINDS.

THEY HAVE SUFFERED A SELF-DIRECTED AGGRESSION FROM INSIDE THEMSELVES.

The buffer group of Independents, notably Donald Winnicott, began to make original contributions of their own and to mark a distinctive character for the group. They were usually people who had been greatly influenced by Melanie Klein, although they repudiated some of her theories.

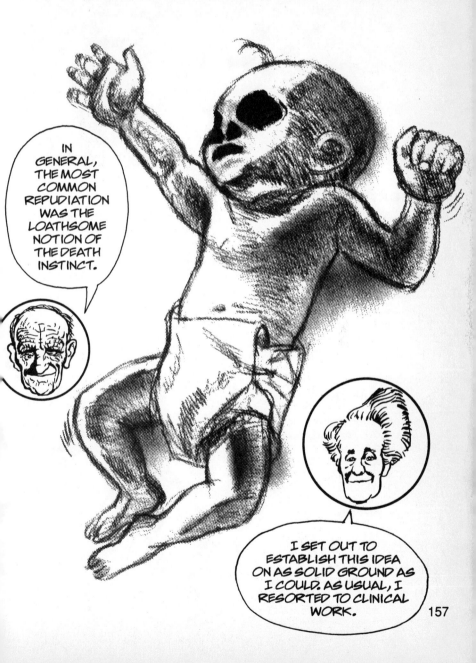

IN GENERAL, THE MOST COMMON REPUDIATION WAS THE LOATHSOME NOTION OF THE DEATH INSTINCT.

I SET OUT TO ESTABLISH THIS IDEA ON AS SOLID GROUND AS I COULD. AS USUAL, I RESORTED TO CLINICAL WORK.

157

The vituperative opposition from Edward Glover and Melitta Schmideberg had vanished when Glover gave up his membership of the British Psycho-Analytical Society in 1944 and Melitta moved to America.

Many students came forward to train with Melanie Klein and her colleagues. Some ten years after she described the paranoid-schizoid position, Klein had re-established herself as the central figure in her own enlarging group. No longer the Society as a whole, but now specifically a Klein group.

Anna Freud's group was also attracting many students and received a lot of research money, particularly from America. She avoided threatening the integrity of the Psycho-Analytical Society and restricted herself largely to the separate institution she set up for child psychotherapy research and training, The Hampstead Clinic.

Klein's Work on Envy

During the 1950s, Melanie Klein wrote a great deal, most notably two long papers. "On Identification" developed the notion of projective identification with many examples from clinical practice, everyday life and literature. The second paper became a book, **Envy and Gratitude** (1957), and was Klein's last great theoretical contribution. It was also the last straw for many other analysts who had tried to keep up with her developments. Donald Winnicott, who was always extremely respectful of Melanie Klein's work, could not stomach the notion of envy.

INSTEAD OF KLEIN'S IDEA OF INNATE AGGRESSION AND ENVY, ALL AGGRESSION COMES FROM AN ACTUAL INCLEMENT ENVIRONMENT THAT DOES NOT FACILITATE THE PHYSICAL OR PSYCHOLOGICAL DEVELOPMENT ADEQUATELY.

TO THIS DAY, "ENVY" IS A BADGE INDICATING WHO BELONGS AND DOES NOT BELONG TO THE KLEIN GROUP.

159

What, therefore, is the importance of Klein's contentious idea of **envy**?

Melanie Klein remained impressed throughout her life by the "quantities" of aggression in the human being.

> CHILDREN SEEM BESET BY VERY VIOLENT PHANTASIES OF AGGRESSION WITHIN THE FAMILY, AND AGONIZINGLY ENGAGED WITH SUPPRESSING IT.

> SERIOUSLY DISTURBED ADULTS REVEAL THE DEVASTATING INTENSITY AND FREQUENCY OF SELF-DIRECTED VIOLENCE AS THEY DESTROY THEIR OWN MINDS.

The notion of envy was Melanie Klein's attempt to understand how the immature and developing mind of the infant tries to deal with an internal state of self-destruction and to mobilize in some way the other side of its nature.

160

Melanie Klein's follower Hanna Segal later described the self-destructive quality of the death instinct, exemplified in Jack London's novel *Martin Eden*. Martin attempts suicide by drowning, but automatically tries to swim. "It was the automatic instinct to live. He ceased swimming, but the moment he felt water rising above his mouth, his hands struck out sharply with a lifting movement."

THIS IS THE WILL TO LIVE . . .

Martin's thought is accompanied by a sneer, vividly captured by London, which dramatically points to the hatred and contempt Martin feels for that wish to go on living. As he drowns, Martin has a tearing pain in the chest. "'The hurt was not death' was the thought that oscillated through his reeling consciousness. It was life – the pangs of life – this awful suffocating feeling. It was the last blow life could deal him." In order for life to continue, that drive towards death has to be painfully combated. The death instinct attacks life itself – for the sake of its liveliness. It is going on living that is painful.

Defining Envy

In order for the infant to survive, the primordial self-directed form of destructiveness has to be dealt with in some way – urgently and immediately. Melanie Klein observed that the first method the infant uses is to direct its hatred of life towards another live object. It combats its own self-destructiveness by directing it elsewhere, towards another object that stands for life and liveliness – and especially the object that seeks to keep the baby alive. Such an object is represented in the first instance by the mother, or more specifically for the infant, the bit of her that it knows best, her breast.

THE ATTACK, FOR ITS OWN SAKE, ON THE LIFE AND GOODNESS OF ANOTHER PERSON IS "ENVY".

This immediate externalization of the death instinct results in phantasies of sucking the life out of something, scooping out the goodness in a form of raiding, stealing, breaking-and-entering.

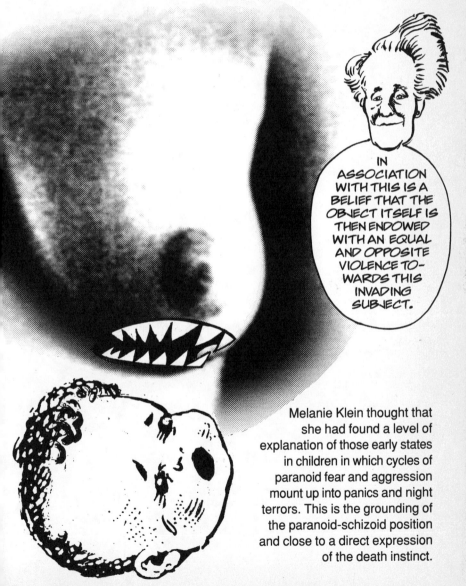

IN ASSOCIATION WITH THIS IS A BELIEF THAT THE OBJECT ITSELF IS THEN ENDOWED WITH AN EQUAL AND OPPOSITE VIOLENCE TOWARDS THIS INVADING SUBJECT.

Melanie Klein thought that she had found a level of explanation of those early states in children in which cycles of paranoid fear and aggression mount up into panics and night terrors. This is the grounding of the paranoid-schizoid position and close to a direct expression of the death instinct.

Melanie Klein's Death

Not long after this, Melanie collapsed on holiday in the summer of 1960. She was brought back home by one of her most devoted colleagues, **Esther Bick** (1901–83). (Bick sought to corroborate Klein's views by observation of infants with their mothers in the very earliest days of life.)

Cancer was diagnosed. Following an operation, Melanie, as always headstrong, fell out of bed and broke her hip. This led to complications from which she did not recover. Melanie Klein died on 22 September 1960. Betty Joseph (another innovative follower of Klein) says that finally, even in the hospital, Melanie was intent on exploring the experience of death. She was "hungry for experience" and was blessed with many, not least of which were the great satisfactions she gained from her work.

Melanie Klein's Continuing Legacy

Melanie Klein had worked to promote her ideas right to the end. She was still restlessly seeking out new ways of presenting them and searching for ways to make her theory more consistent. She left a devoted group of students and colleagues. It is to her credit that her restlessness lived on in the vibrant efforts to develop her work, to form a body of coherent knowledge, to explore new ways of working with intractable patients and to inspire future generations of students.

Melanie Klein was for the major part of her career a British psychoanalyst. Her ideas were very much the product of the British Psycho-Analytical Society. Psychoanalysts from other countries frequently came to Britain to train with her and her group. There are now groups of Kleinian analysts in many other countries. Interest in Klein's work is increasing in most of the major psychoanalytic centres in the world.

Klein and Group Therapy

Klein's ideas have proved particularly adaptable to application in many settings other than the rigorous psychoanalytic consulting room. And this has occurred despite Melanie Klein's own persistent rigour in sticking to her analytic technique. There have been many ways in which her ideas and the developments of her followers have been taken up in wider academic and cultural discourses. Largely because of the interpersonal aspects of her concept of projective identification, Klein's ideas have fertilized other forms of psychotherapy, notably group therapy. The processes involved in projective identification are deeply embedded in social life, perhaps its bedrock.

Projective identification occurs in groups and may even be the process that welds individuals into groups. This is why group behaviour tends to be so primitive. The projection of parts of the ego into others in the social environment can result in one person being the receptacle for similar projections from the others, with a forcefully defined unconscious role to play for the whole group. History has made us familiar with this phenomenon. Guilt is projected into one person who then takes on the role of scapegoat. Much of this extension of Klein's work into the social sphere has been undertaken at the Tavistock Clinic in London, initiated by Wilfred Bion and other followers, such as Isabel Menzies and Elliott Jaques.

Klein and Feminism

Melanie Klein emphasized the role
of the mother as the important figure.
This has made Kleinian ideas both
congenial and accessible to a strand
of Feminist thought in Britain and
internationally. Juliet Mitchell, arguably
the most important contemporary
Feminist in Britain to mine Freud for
ideas on the gender differences
between men and women, turned in
the 1980s to Melanie Klein's writing for
even earlier psychological determinants
of social genders.

Klein and Lacan

Much academic interest in
psychoanalysis was instigated by the
theories of **Jacques Lacan** (1901–81).
Because of Lacan's idea of the rule of
le nom du père (the name of the
father), many Lacanians too have
sought out the more balanced
perspective that Melanie Klein achieved
in stressing the mother – and the role of
both father and mother in the
168 "combined parent figure".

Melanie Klein's final gift to us was the posthumous publication of a session-by-session account of an analysis, entitled **Narrative of a Child Analysis**. This is the story of Richard's analysis. He was the boy we met earlier who (like Mrs Klein's followers) learned to keep her as his lifelong friend by keeping her securely alive forever inside him.

Further Reading

Hanna Segal, **Klein**, Fontana Modern Masters, London 1979.
This is an accessible account by one of Klein's most prominent followers. It is a clear technical introduction with some historical and biographical context. This is the ideal next step in your acquaintance with Melanie Klein.

R.D. Hinshelwood, **Clinical Klein**, Free Association Books, London 1994; Jason Aronson, New York 1994.
This book illustrates Klein's discoveries and concepts by using the clinical material that she and her followers presented as evidence. It will explain to you each step in the clinical process, the clinician's thinking and how it resulted in theoretical developments.

Julia Segal, **Phantasy in Everyday Life**, Penguin, London 1985; Jason Aronson, New York 1995.
This is an easily accessible account of the Kleinian understanding of the unconscious mind as it appears in ordinary everyday life. Be aware that the many small but familiar examples will suggest that you too operate at these disturbing levels of the mind.

Juliet Mitchell (ed.), **The Selected Papers of Melanie Klein**, Penguin, London 1986; The Free Press, New York 1987.
Juliet Mitchell gives a brief and often lucid introduction to each of the classic papers in her selection from Klein's work. You might have hoped that Klein's two papers written for the lay person – "Weaning" and "Love, Guilt and Reparation" – would have been published here, but they will have to be consulted in Volume 1 of **The Writings of Melanie Klein**, Hogarth, London 1975 (reprinted by Virago); The Free Press, New York 1984.

Phyllis Grosskurth, **Melanie Klein: Her World and Her Work**, Hodder & Stoughton, London 1986; Harvard University Press, Cambridge, Mass. 1987.
To date the best biography. It is absorbing to read about Klein's often distressing but creative life. Technical explanations of her work are less reliable. A stage play – *Mrs Klein* – was based on some of this biography, written by Nicholas Wright, Nick Hern, London 1988.

James and Alix Strachey (ed. Perry Meisel and Walter Kendrick), **Bloomsbury/Freud**, Chatto & Windus, London 1985.
This is the correspondence in 1924 when Alix Strachey in Berlin (for an analysis with Karl Abraham) and her husband James, in London, wrote to each other nearly every day. They give a wonderful evocation, drenched with dry English humour, of the psychoanalytic world in Berlin where Melanie Klein was developing her work with children, and the London world where the Bloomsbury group and the Stracheys' psychoanalytic colleagues were getting to know each other.

Little Dictionary and Index

Acknowledgements

Robert Hinshelwood and Susan Robinson would like to thank Richard Appignanesi for his work in shaping the text so perfectly to Oscar's wonderful drawings, and Duncan Heath for his meticulous copy-editing.

Oscar Zarate would like to thank Bahue Aranovich, Alicia Arendar, Madeleine Fenton, Judy Groves, Hazel Hirshorn, Zoran Jevtic, Marta Rodriguez and Morgan Zarate for their invaluable help and support in the making of this book.

Typesetting by **Wayzgoose**
Handlettering by **Woodrow Phoenix**

Photo Credits
Page 3: Dr Hans Thorner
Page 119: Wellcome Institute Library, London

Robert Hinshelwood is a psychoanalyst and Clinical Director of The Cassel Hospital in London. He founded the *International Journal of Therapeutic Communities* and the *British Journal of Psychotherapy*. His other books include *A Dictionary of Kleinian Thought* and *Clinical Klein*.

Susan Robinson began work as a psychosocial nurse at The Cassel Hospital in 1987, and since 1994 she has been the Head Nurse there.

Oscar Zarate has illustrated six other *Beginners* books: *Freud, Stephen Hawking, Lenin, Mafia, Machiavelli* and *Quantum Theory*. He has also produced many acclaimed graphic novels, including *A Small Killing*, which won the Will Eisner Prize for the best graphic novel of 1994, and has edited *It's Dark in London*, a collection of graphic stories, published in 1996.

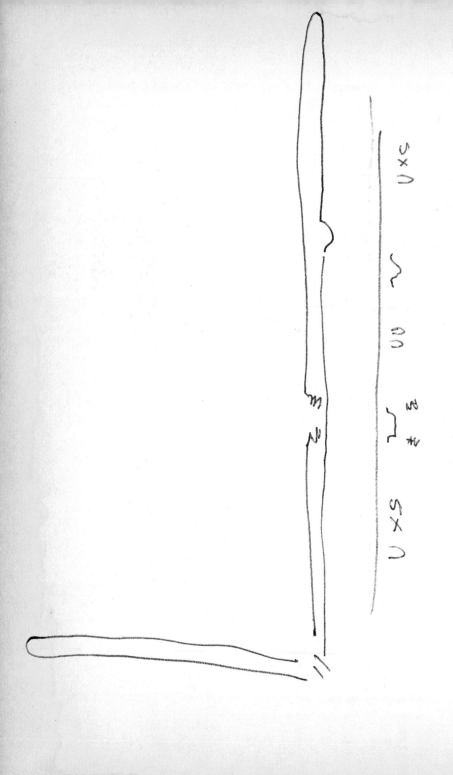